The Great Land Grab

Michael Bachelard was a parliamentary and Aboriginal affairs correspondent for *The Canberra Times* in the period preceding the momentous Wik judgment of December 1996. This dual role gave him a unique opportunity to meet and interview all sides in the native title debate, and to gain an in-depth understanding of the politicking in Canberra. In travelling to remote communities in Arnhem Land and central Australia, he also acquired an appreciation of the concerns of Aboriginal and non-Aboriginal people caught up in the fracas.

He now pursues his career as a journalist in Melbourne. *The Great Land Grab* is his first book.

The
Great Land Grab

*What
Every Australian Should Know
About WIK, MABO and
the TEN-POINT PLAN*

Michael Bachelard

HYLAND HOUSE

First published in Australia in 1997 by
Hyland House Publishing Pty Ltd
Hyland House
387–389 Clarendon Street
South Melbourne
Victoria 3205

Revised editions 1997, 1998

National Library of Australia
Cataloguing-in-publication data:

Bachelard, Michael, 1968–.
The great land grab: what every Australian should know about Wik, Mabo and the ten-point plan.

Includes index.
ISBN 1 86447 031 3.

1. Australia. High Court. Mabo and others v. State of Queensland. 2. Australia. High Court. Wik peoples v. State of Queensland and others. 3. Australia. Native Title Act 1993. 4. Native title. I. Title.

346.940432

Typeset in Caslon 11/12pt by Hyland House
Printed by Australian Print Group, Maryborough, Victoria

Foreword by Patrick Dodson

The importance of giving Australians knowledge to make informed judgements on matters fundamental to the nature of who we are as a people can never be underestimated. There are some issues that have to be beyond ideology and Aboriginal Land Justice fits firmly into this category. A nation that ignores the rights to fundamental justice to any group of its people will be harshly judged by history, and a mean-spirited approach to the land aspirations of Indigenous Australians will only diminish us as a nation in the eyes of a watching world.

No one can pretend that the matter of Native Title, Wik and Mabo are not complex matters that require a wisdom and vision for the future that we Australians often find difficult to muster. But this effort to put the issue into a form that allows all Australians, no matter what their level of experience in the arena, is an important step in informing young Australians, in particular, of the complexities. I encourage you to read and make judgements based on the balance that this document attempts to provide.

Patrick Dodson

Foreword by Cheryl Kernot

When the High Court handed down its decisions in both the Mabo and Wik cases, it also handed the nation an opportunity. That opportunity was for reconciliation with indigenous Australia. Despite indigenous people being amongst the most impoverished citizens of this country, some others have seen the Wik decision as an opportunity to grind the racist axe and further their own political and financial agendas. Native title is one of the most complex areas of the law, but it's also an area where simple generosity of spirit can and should prevail. Michael Bachelard has captured the essence of the debate so far and has struck a balance between the necessary legal background and a responsible social commentary. It is refreshing to see a balanced perspective. *The Great Land Grab: What Every Australian Should Know about Wik, Mabo and the Ten-point plan* is essential reading for all Australians who care about where we are going as a nation and what sort of country we want our children to inherit.

Cheryl Kernot

Foreword by
Jack Waterford

The High Court's decision in the Mabo case was a landmark in Australian history. The court struck out two centuries of a legal lie—the assumption that the land upon which British colonists had settled was an empty land, or one occupied only by barbarians.

The abolition of the legal fiction was a great moral victory for Aborigines, but whether and to what extent it provided fresh opportunities for them was a matter of considerable debate. There were some whose fury at the decision seemed based merely on resentment about the overthrow of settled, if plainly false, jurisprudence. But there were other non-Aboriginal Australians who feared that the decision could affect their power and control over land which they occupied. A highly emotive and misleading campaign suggested that not even suburban backyards might be safe from an Aboriginal land claim. This was plainly nonsense. Everywhere there had been extensive urban or rural settlement of Australia, the way in which titles had been granted had shown a clear intention to pass over to landholders clear titles which admitted no possibility of continuing Aboriginal legal interest.

But in the most remote parts of Australia there were continuing question marks.

In the long debate over the Native Title Bill, one of the most persistent demands of farming interests was that any such continuing rights, if they existed at all, be extinguished. This the Keating Government was reluctant to do. If such rights had persisted for more than 200 years, it would seem particularly unfair that a further act of colonial settlement – brought on by the first recognition since that settlement that native title could persist –should steal it away. Aboriginal groups should have their opportunity to establish any continuing rights they did have.

The propaganda of grazing interest has continually insisted that the threat of native title is to battler farmers and graziers in reasonable closely settled areas. In fact, in most of the lands which could be subjected to native title claims, the land holdings are enormous, running into hundreds, and sometimes thousands of square kilometres. The major landholders are among Australia's richest companies and Australia's richest men and women. In much of this country, the pattern of non-Aboriginal land use has been desultory at best, often typified by non-owner occupation, a heavy reliance on (and, for decades, exploitation of) Aboriginal labour and, often, persistent failure to carry out terms of leases.

The Wik claim was chosen as being amongst the most arguable which could be put up. As Michael Bachelard documents in this very valuable primer to the argument, the pattern of dealings in this land showed little or no 'occupation' by non-Aborigines. The only continuity was the presence, and continued care and attention to the land, of its original owners – a presence which ample evidence showed had been contemplated by all who had been involved in the dealings with the land.

But the result of the Wik decision has been treated as a disaster by pastoral interests, and by conservative state governments. They have redoubled efforts to get a flat legislative extinguishment of all such claims, in the process making many misleading, alarmist, and sometimes racist, arguments about the decision's effect. The Howard Government has attempted to give an impression of steering a middle path between the different interests, but as this book demonstrates, its Ten Point Plan, if enacted, serves as an effective extinguishment of Aboriginal rights.

In fact, it will be perhaps the more effective for achieving the result indirectly.

The ordinary citizen, attempting through this primer, to sort through the propaganda and false alarms might notice several features which go well beyond some mere dispute about competing claims for land.

One is that there is every appearance of an agenda on the part of those most vociferously demanding extinguishment which has little to do with Aborigines at all. They want to exchange their limited leasehold tenure of their land for clear title which puts no restriction whatever on their rights. They do not not want to pay for it. They have been tenants, allowed to live on land subject to the payment of small rents, and to use it for limited purposes. The history of that land use, leaving quite aside issues of their treatment of Aborigines or any continuing interests Aborigines may have – has been a quite unhappy one: it is, often, a story of poor land management, overstocking, failure to properly maintain the land in poor seasons, and the creation, actively or by neglect, of a vast environmental disaster. Because of the political power of some of the interests involved, government has done little about it by strict enforcement of the leases. The demand now is that government deprive itself of most of the power it has to do so, and that it sacrifice rights, interests and value which it hold in trust for all Australians, including Aboriginal Australians, and appropriates it to big landholders for little value. That the 'emergency' creating the need for 'certainty' happens to be the risk of Aboriginal land claims could almost be an accident. The land grab that the Ten Points could authorise would make the actions of the squatter in the first half of the nineteenth century minor by comparison.

The second thing which the reader will note is that the climate of dealing properly with the rights and aspirations of Aboriginal interests has changed, and apparently in fundamental ways. It has been only for about 30 years that Aboriginal aspirations have had much public sympathy. It was only about 20 years ago that this sympathy became a relatively bipartisan one. Now, however, the Prime Minister has declared that he believes that the pendulum has swung too far in the direction of Aborigines and that it is time to put it back. Aboriginal programs have been severely pruned. And, if the Ten Point Plan is implemented, Aboriginal rights will have been deliberately reduced. For those, such as myself, who mark Aboriginal advancement not only by indices of wellbeing and material improvement (and here the situation is so depressing that it deserves another book) but also by psychological steps and landmarks, the signal seems very ominous. Ominous not only for Aboriginal Australians but for others who think that our citizenship and our nation is diminished while we suffer such material and moral disadvantage to persist.

But even more depressing is the evidence that the Labor Party may no longer have the will to continue to promote the old bipartisan approach. It has not, so far, disavowed it, but it seems that it has detected the unpopularity that any high-profile or moral leadership might bring and would like to 'de-emphasise' its commitment there.

In this book, Michael Bachelard has very successfully negotiated the complicated story, presenting a history and an explanation of the legal arguments and the implications of alternative policy directions. He has listened to all sides, and, if he plainly prefers some versions to others, he has explained carefully and fairly the alternative views. His book shows a professionalism but also a passion which I would expect from such a journalist – one who has taken the trouble not only to read the materials and to talk to those involved, but also to have visited Aboriginal communities and pastoral enterprises and to have come to know the actors. This book is an essential companion to the debate going on.

Jack Waterford
Editor
The Canberra Times

Contents

Acknowledgements

Thanks must go first to Jack Waterford who, as the editor of *The Canberra Times* and one of the most knowledgeable people I have met, first encouraged my interest in Aboriginal affairs. Martin Freckmann, ATSIC's media adviser and a hoarder of newspaper articles, was a great resource, as were Liz Westcott and others from ATSIC and land councils around the country. Rick Farley and Frank Brennan make difficult concepts easy to understand, Phillip Hunter set me straight on a number of things, and Kate Schulze was a great help. The staff at *The Canberra Times* library made efforts beyond the call of duty. Thanks to Cheryl Thurlow, Cheryl Kernot, Patrick Dodson, Paul Lane and Daryl Melham, who all took time out from busy lives to help. Joan Grant and Sonia Smallacombe both made invaluable suggestions. The interviewees, Bill Taylor, Carol Kendall, Ewan Vickery, Francis Yunkaporta, Joy Marriott, Mary-Lou Buck and Will Roberts, put the people in the story. Very special thanks to Andrew Wilkins, friend and publisher.

Finally, to Sally Paxton, who became my wife during the writing of this book and who means everything to me, thank you, my wild grapevine.

LAND USE IN AUSTRALIA

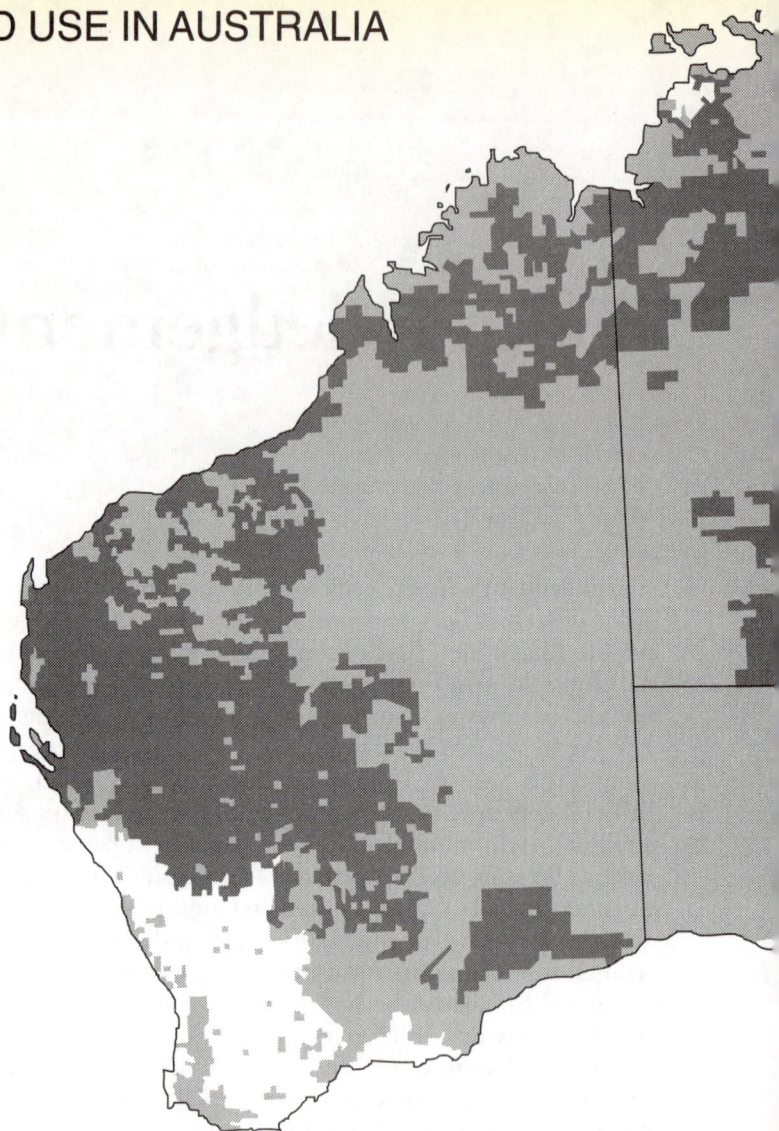

Mainly freehold

Vacant Crown land, Aboriginal land,
or forestry reserves and national parks

Pastoral lease land

Source: Bureau of Resource Sciences

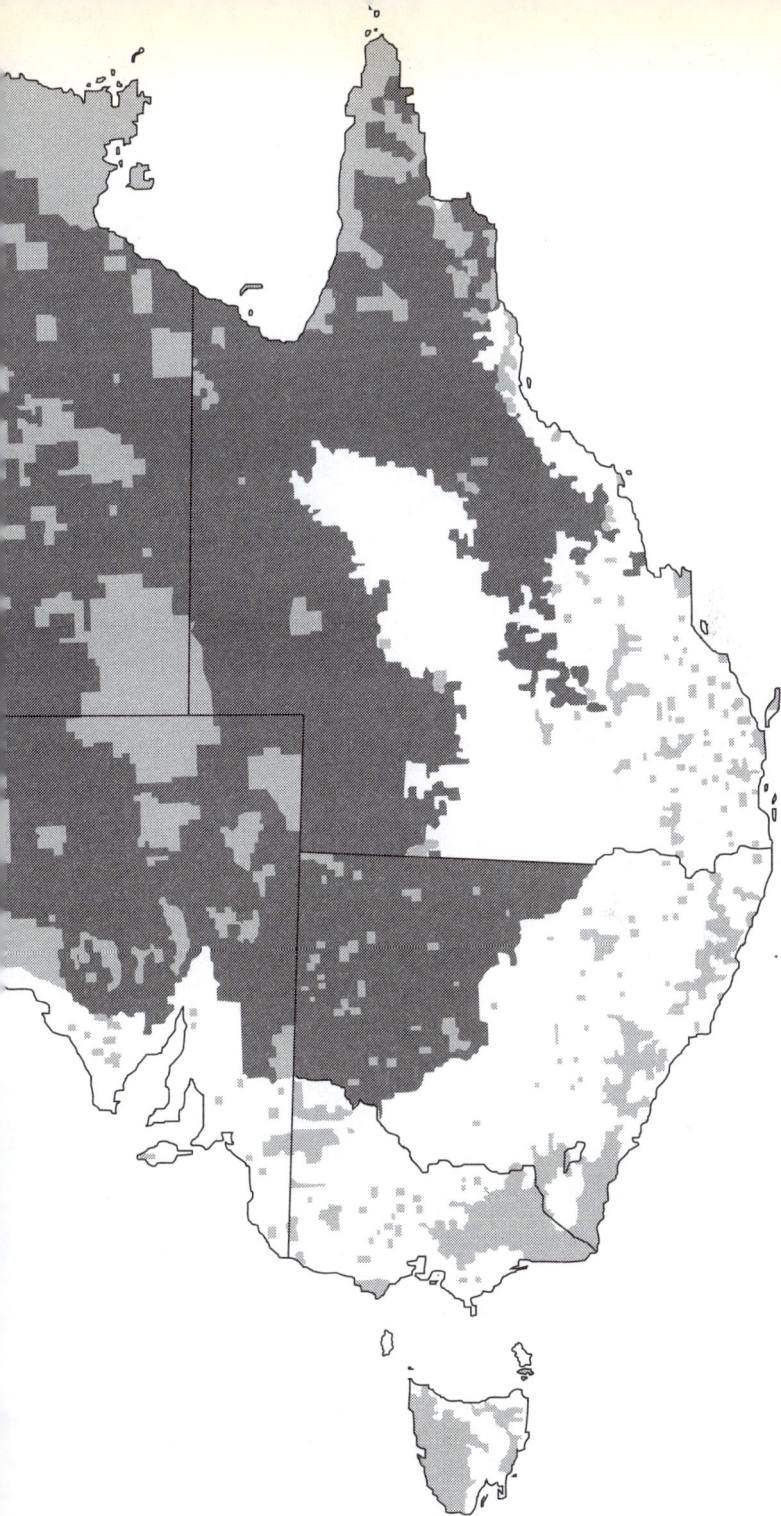

Introduction

Gladys Tybingoompa danced for joy outside the High Court on 23 December 1996.

'Out of here we go, no one being a loser,' she said through her grin.

Australians around the country saw her celebration on the TV news, and knew that, once again, the High Court had done something important for Aboriginal people.

Just five months later another image, filmed in black and white, appeared on the nation's TVs.

Two young children, one Aboriginal and one blond and freckly, were playing Twister on a black and white board. A sinister soundtrack, like wind blowing across a desert, filled the background as the boys spun the pointer and competed for territory.

This game was no fun. Their movements were urgent, their faces serious. Sometimes the black boy won a round, sometimes the white boy. At the end they both tumbled to the ground.

'Can Black and White Australians live in harmony when the High Court's Wik decision on native title has created uncertainty, especially for farmers?' the voice-over asked in grave tones. 'Whose land is it? Who can use it? Farmers want their rights restored and control of their future.

'The Wik decision – it's not a game.'

A second advertisement, this time in harsh colour, showed a farmer clutching a heavy post to his chest with his work-scarred hands. The white blindfold he was wearing thwarted his attempts to put the post in a hole in the red, drought-parched earth. His frustration was clear. His family looked on helplessly.

'Working the land is hard enough,' said the voice. 'The High Court's Wik decision has made it even tougher.'

The Wik Peoples v. The State of Queensland & Others. It has prompted more public debate, more newspaper articles, more political hair-tearing than any average Australian could be expected to keep track of. What was it about? How did it come to be in the High Court? How does it relate to the Mabo decision of 1992 and the *Native Title Act* of 1993? Whom does it really benefit? At what cost? How are our leaders coming to terms with it? These are the questions Australians have been fighting about since Gladys Tybingoompa did her celebration dance on that sunny summer's day in Canberra. And they are the questions tackled in this book.

But why do we need to know about these things?

Just months after the swearing in of the Howard Government in March 1996, Australia's most respected Aboriginal leaders were declaring a crisis in Aboriginal affairs. The new Government's funding cuts to the Aboriginal and Torres Strait Islander Commission, the onerous accountability requirements aimed at Aboriginal organisations, and the perceived neglect of the reconciliation process all conspired to undermine the respect of the Aboriginal community for those in charge in Canberra.

It is a crisis Aborigines do not need. They have already lost most of their land, their right to self-determination and, in some cases, their dignity. Their interactions with a white society which would neither let them live as they always had nor let them live as equals, has conspired to erode their health and their social cohesion on a massive scale. They have the highest rates of imprisonment in the land, they die in custody at much higher rates than other Australians. Outside jail they still die 17 years, on average, younger than white Australians. Many young Aborigines are estranged from their culture and ancestral languages, and face high unemployment and an uncertain future.

But while indigenous relations with the Government might have been at crisis point, there has been some evidence of a countervailing shift in the national attitude. White Australia has been gradually awakening in the past 30 years to the extent of Aboriginal dispossession. The path to this new recognition has been peppered by memorable moments – the overwhelming support for the 1967 referendum that gave Aboriginal people the vote, Gough Whitlam pouring sand into Vincent Lingiari's hand, Malcolm Fraser shepherding the 1976 *Northern Territory Land Rights Act* through Parliament, the protests at the Bicentenary in 1988, Paul Keating's speech at Redfern when he acknowledged the extent of Aboriginal pain, and now the High Court's Mabo and Wik decisions.

The new recognition is reflected in the strong community response to reports like *Bringing Them Home*, tabled in July 1997, which told heart-rending stories about the stolen generations of Aboriginal children, and in the widespread support for the process of reconciliation.

How we approach relations with indigenous Australians is one of the most important issues that we face as we move towards further landmark events – a republic, when we make the symbolic break with our colonial past, the centenary of Federation and the new millennium. More than anything else our approach to reconciliation and native title will shape our reputation on human rights in the international arena.

Many of the attempts to deal with these issues until now have failed. We have poured money in to fix problems we have not adequately understood. We have tried policies ranging from genocide to assimilation, self-determination, reconciliation and economic empowerment. Just as the High Court in the Wik case provides the signpost to how we might coexist in Australia's heartland, we find that heartland being swayed by the preachings of Pauline Hanson, who has lent an extreme edge to the debate.

But whatever paths these grand movements in the national psyche take, we need to understand the facts of that case.

Many people's knowledge is limited to the images presented in John Singleton's Twister ads for the National Farmers' Federation. These 30-second grabs graphically illustrated one side of the debate, provoking emotions and making their point clearly and forcefully. But they did it by invoking fear – they showed threatening images, competitive images, images of frustration, anxiety, impending disaster.

It is a fear that has pervaded the farming community and beyond.

'Tell the politicians we need legislation to sort out the mess and get it right. For the sake of black and white,' the ads said.

The politicians responded. John Howard formulated his plan.

And there can be no doubt that his 10-point solution overturns aspects of the High Court's judgement. It has the potential to allow pastoralists, aided by state governments and paid for mainly by taxpayers, to make a land grab the like of which has not been seen since the battles last century for Australia's territory. In those conflicts indigenous people were driven away from their ancestral country at gunpoint as the nation expanded and pursued pasture and gold. Will they be driven away again, this time by legislation?

Or will we all be able to dance together at the end of this, 'no one being a loser'?

1

Matters of History

What is native title?

Legal fictions

It was all so easy before Eddie Mabo came along.

Australian governments and courts had a perfectly workable and consistent system of land law and tenure which, despite the inevitable disputes and occasional modifications, had stood them in good stead since 1788. In other words, they had certainty.

Aborigines had very little of anything, but that, it seemed, was just the way it had to be.

Under the system of law that existed before 3 June 1992, the various governments of Australia, known (because they derived their authority from the king or queen of England) as the Crown, were authorised first by the colonial power of Britain and then under the power of the Commonwealth of Australia to make laws for all their subjects on this new land. The British common law, it was said, was one of the birthrights of the English, even if they were colonists settling the outer reaches of the empire.

Under this system of law, settling a place that was *terra nullius* – land belonging to nobody – was easy. Sovereignty was acquired when such land was occupied. The rights of the existing inhabitants, in this case Aboriginal and Torres Strait Islander Australians, counted for nothing because under British law they were officially recognised only as barbarians, and in need of the boon of civilisation and white society.

Their existing societies, their laws and customs, which were varied and complex, were ignored by the colonists, who were blind to their existence.

Among the prerogatives the Crown allowed itself when it assumed control of this continent in 1788 was the ability to sell and distribute land. The right to do this was acquired, in common law, under a feudal legal doctrine which held that all lands in Britain were the property of the sovereign. In theory, the king or queen had absolute ownership of the land, and could give permission to whomever he or she wanted to occupy it. The occupier was merely a tenant of the sovereign.

This feudal system of land tenure was a legal fiction that was just about irrelevant in England by 1788 before it was revived, for the sake of convenience, for the purposes of settling and populating the colonies.

In its colonial setting the tenure system allowed the Crown, in one act, to award itself what was called 'radical title' (ultimate or final title) over the whole of Australia. Its representatives, the colonial administrators and governments, had the ability to dispose of the land as they saw fit, in the name of the Crown and of civilisation.

For governments, landholders and lawyers this made things quite straightforward. As High Court Justice Michael Kirby pointed out in the Wik case, the land tenure system had a 'unifying simplicity to commend it: No legally enforceable rights to land pre-existing annexation and settlement'.[1]

If anybody stopped to think of the various legal fictions on which tenure was based – including the failure to recognise Aboriginal rights – such thoughts were dismissed until now because the weight of history, the volumes of legal reasoning, and the need for certainty decreed that it be so.

It was this doctrine that allowed white settlement (or invasion, depending on your perspective) to begin at the coastal colonies and mushroom into almost every remote corner of the country. Under the impact of its expansion Aboriginal people were rounded up and removed from their land and their waterholes poisoned. They were given poisoned flour, or often were simply shot as though they were vermin. Some indigenous inhabitants retaliated with violence, but their land continued to be appropriated. In some areas their presence was tolerated, or they were rounded up and used for cheap labour and sex by the pioneers, creating a growing population of so-called 'half-castes'.

Government policy oscillated from ignoring their presence to trying to assimilate them and giving (at least tacit) approval of their extermination. No matter which policy was currently in force, their land was sold out from under them without their being consulted or compensated.

A legal revolution

The whole system worked very well for the white settlers, and very much to their advantage, right up until Eddie Mabo and the Meriam people of Murray Island came along in 1992 and forced the High Court to look carefully at it.

Until then it had been assumed that the Crown's radical title conferred on the federal government and the states and territories the right to full beneficial ownership of the land. Such ownership ruled out the prospect of any other people using the land or living on it. It assumed that the English common law recognised only the right of an individual to own land, not a right of group ownership.

What the High Court did in the Mabo judgement was to find that in the Torres Strait, radical title had by no means overridden the Meriam people's right to continue to live on their island, cultivating their gardens, tending their fish traps and settling disputes using their own complex system of law.

It must follow, the court found, that the Crown's radical title was not the same thing as full ownership, and did not preclude Torres Strait Islanders, or, by analogy, Aborigines on the mainland, having a legal title to the land.

As Justice Gerard Brennan pointed out in his landmark judgement in *Mabo*, the power to make rules governing land distribution is an entirely different thing from the ownership of the land itself. While a sovereign, the Crown, might have the right to distribute land for others to use, it is a nonsense to say in England that the monarch owns all the land as his or her actual property, and in Australia that governments themselves can own, use and enjoy the vast areas of land over which they have radical title.[2]

On this basis, and with a clear sense of justice that surpassed mere legalism and tradition, Brennan and five of his fellow judges ruled that the doctrine of *terra nullius* was an offensive legal fiction, that the Crown's radical title gave it the right to distribute land but not the right to absolute beneficial ownership of it, and that, in the absence of such ownership, the prior and continuing group ownership of land by Australia's Aboriginal and Torres Strait Islander inhabitants must be recognised by the common law which had ignored it for so long.

It was a revolution in legal thinking.

Brennan himself was not so emotive, but said much the same thing: 'The facts as we know them today do not fit the "absence of law" or "barbarian" theory underpinning the colonial reception of the common law of England. That being so, there is no warrant for applying in these times rules of the English common law which were the product of that theory. It would be a curious doctrine to propound today that, when the benefit of the common law was first extended to Her Majesty's indigenous subjects in the Antipodes, its first fruits were to strip them of their right to occupy their ancestral lands.'[3]

Common law recognition

However, the High Court's decision was not so revolutionary that the judges threw out the whole common law of Australia as it related to land title. Even though the system was built on fictions that would be offensive to modern Australian standards of justice, Brennan said the court was not free to adopt *any* rules in the name of justice or human rights 'if their adoption would fracture the skeleton of principle which gives the body of our law its shape and internal consistency'.[4]

Rather than overturning the whole concept of property in Australia (Brennan conceded it was 'far too late in the day' for that), the court postulated that the common law could and should recognise that indigenous people still had a right to live on their land, hunt and fish there, and conduct their ceremonies. This right, where it still existed, the High Court called 'native title'. Its survival was possible because, despite the activities of the colonists, some Aboriginal and Torres Strait Islander people still lived on their land and had done so continuously since settlement. The customs of the Meriam people, for example, had survived as a coherent system of laws, based in tradition.

'Where a clan or group has continued to acknowledge the laws and (so far as practicable) to observe the customs based on the traditions of that clan or group, whereby their traditional connexion with the land has been substantially maintained, the traditional community title of that clan or group can be said to remain in existence. The common law can, by reference to the traditional laws and customs of an indigenous people, identify and protect the native rights and interests to which they give rise,' Brennan wrote.[5]

In other words native title existed not as a creation of the British common law, but as something the common law recognised as being a valid legal and customary system in itself – a system which could live alongside the common law.

The decision meant that native title rights were actually enforceable as rights under the common law. Australian courts had an obligation to recognise and defend them against attack but they existed even without such recognition by a court.

'That is what is meant when it is said that native title is recognised by the common law,' Brennan said in his Wik judgement. 'Unless traditional law or custom so requires, native title does not require any conduct on the part of any person to complete it, nor does it depend for its existence on any legislative, executive or judicial declaration.'[6]

Extinguishment
However, in its attempt to recognise native title without overturning the skeleton of the common law, the High Court had to deal with the reality of 204 years of history. In practice, this meant that most past actions were found to be valid, and native title was restricted to parts of Australia known as 'vacant Crown lands' – land not ever settled.

This meant, despite the fear-mongering of conservative forces after the decision, that Australian backyards and city streets were safe from claims. This was the case even though they had become backyards and city streets on the shaky foundations of conquest, settlement and the tenure system of land law. The High Court was realistic enough to recognise that by 1992 the land had been appropriated, parcel by parcel, and could not be given back.

To ensure the security of tenures granted legally in the past, the Court talked in terms of the 'extinguishment' of native title. The Court ruled that certain historical events had performed this extinguishment. The first was that indigenous people could lose their native title if they lost connection with their land and law, since only through these connections had the common law recognised their native title. The flame of native title could also be snuffed out by three major acts of governments: by laws which simply and directly extinguished it; by laws which created rights in third parties that were inconsistent with the continued right to enjoy it (for example, the sale of land into freehold and the building of a house or a government utility on it); and by laws through which the Crown directly and clearly upgraded its radical title over land to full ownership.

Writing of extinguishment in his Wik judgement, Brennan said the strength of native title was 'that it is enforceable by the ordinary courts. Its weakness is that it is not an estate held from the Crown nor is it protected by the common law as Crown tenures are protected ... Native title is liable to be extinguished by laws enacted by, or with the authority of, the legislature or by the act of the executive in exercise of powers conferred upon it.'[7]

Having put this proviso on the survival of native title, the Court also put various conditions on the powers that could extinguish it.

For example, any act of the Crown's to extinguish native title by simply legislating it out of existence would have to have occurred before the *Racial Discrimination Act* had come into force in 1975. In other words, any government enacting a simple legislative extinguishment of native title on vacant Crown land would be acting in a racially discriminatory way.

That government might have breached Australia's international obligations under racial discrimination conventions, because such an action would override the rights of a group of people where those rights existed exclusively because of their race.

This means that state and territory governments can not override native title on their lands with a flick of the pen, and the Commonwealth can do so only if it first repeals or amends the *Racial Discrimination Act*, or passes another law that is inconsistent with it. Both major parties have ruled this option out (although some on the current Government's backbench would be happy with nothing less) because they fear the political consequences. Besides, with no majority in the Senate this is likely to be very difficult for any government to do.

The High Court's majority judges also left some important issues undecided in their discussion of extinguishment. One was whether the government's grant of a leasehold interest in land (as opposed to freehold) extinguished native title, and another was whether the Crown needed to indicate an awareness that it was extinguishing native title. The judges disagreed on this. Justices Deane, Gaudron and Toohey in *Mabo* thought that if native title was to be extinguished by the Crown granting an inconsistent title to another party (the second route to extinguishment), the Crown needed to express clearly and unambiguously in legislation its wish to extinguish that title. If the Crown did not do so, native title would be assumed to have survived. But if the intention to extinguish had been made clear and this had happened after 1975, it would have been a breach of the *Racial Discrimination Act*, and therefore would attract just-terms compensation to the Aborigines whose rights had been trammelled.

But the majority – Chief Justice Mason and Justices Brennan, McHugh and Dawson – disagreed with this view. Accordingly the Court did not make a ruling on that point, leaving it for later examination.

The Wik case invited an examination of precisely these two aspects of extinguishment. Chapter 2 explains that these were two of the crucial issues on which the Wik decision turned.

'No one knows what's what'

Bill Taylor, pastoralist, 'Lesdale', Charleville, Queensland

' ... I've been 10 years on this place. Before that I was in this district, and I've lived basically in south-west Queensland all my life except for the time I went to school, so that's 53 years ... We've got a grazing homestead perpetual lease. We are hopeful it gives us secure tenure, but that's up to the courts to decide. We don't know. It's still leasehold, so we have got native title claims on our country. They wouldn't accept claims on freehold, but we are told now that there is, well, we are hopeful that when it goes to court a grazing homestead perpetual lease will be treated the same as freehold because we have got what may be termed exclusive tenure and our lease is perpetual ...

'I suppose the big thing is, we don't understand the claim ... No one has come out from any authority and said 'Native title is this, it allows them to do this, or this, or this'. We don't know ... It's not going to push us off the land, no that can't happen ... If it was the worst scenario for us, that they have full access rights and could run around everywhere, the value of the land could drop considerably – we don't know if that would be 5 per cent or 50 per cent ...

'There wouldn't have been any Aboriginals as Aboriginals on this place since it was given out as a lease in 1912. And there probably wouldn't have been any a long time before that. This country was settled in about 1860 or something ... This isn't sort of Aboriginal country. There's no natural water here, you see. We catch our own water in earth dams. If we took our artificial water off this country it would be dry for 90 per cent of the year.

'There's two claims. There's the Gungarri claim, their headquarters is at Mitchell, I really believe it's an ambit claim ... And the other claim is the Bidjara claim ... and I don't

know, they just got a map and ran a pencil around it ...
Basically the claim is in the hands of the courts and the
courts, naturally, are governed by judges and lawyers who
haven't any feel for this country. And they're making what I
call abstract decisions ... It's all up for interpretation by
judges in the High Court. It's not a matter for lay people ...

'I think one of the other things is that people out here
have had it pretty rough in the last six or seven years. We've
had a pretty severe drought but our commodity prices have
probably been worse than our drought, and people who've
had overdrafts had 25 per cent interest rates, so they've had
a triple whammy out in this country. On my own little
operation out here we basically went nearly five years
straight without income and then to come in and get a native
title claim over your place, you know, what's next? ... Most
of the people out here, even if they did have money seven
years ago, most people's financial situation has dropped
alarmingly. There's quite a number of people out here with
desperate problems with money ... desperate to the point
of being fear ...

'And I think people found those comments from people in
the city who hardly know where milk comes from ...
Seriously, I think it was pretty insulting to rural people. And
then I think the fact that the Government sort of put a
blanket on and said there would be no claims over towns or
urban areas – that hurt rural people, because no towns or
infrastructure could be claimed. Sure that's where the people
are and that's where the votes are, but that created a huge
amount of bad feeling. The fact is that there is this void of no
one knows what's what.'

Labor's legislation: *The Native Title Act 1993*

Paul Keating and the then Labor government could have ignored the Mabo judgement. The way native title was described, as a right recognised by the common law, meant any Aboriginal person could take a claim for title to court and have a decision made there. Some Aboriginal leaders preferred this approach – they argued that their people had won far more from the courts than the parliaments over the years.

But three months after the decision was handed down, Keating instituted a consultation process which took a full year to complete. In January of the following year, with an election two months away, he announced he would legislate to give statutory force to the judgement.

Keating realised (as a Coalition government probably also would have) that legislation was necessary to provide a regime that made clear sense to all the various stakeholders. Legislation was the best chance to provide certainty for developers, give full protection for native title, and create a system that was not bogged down in the courts for years to come.

But legislation proved enormously difficult to achieve.

What the negotiation process revealed was a variety of completely contradictory views. On the one side, taking the hardest line, were the state premiers (particularly Western Australia's Richard Court, whose state contains by far the largest area of vacant Crown land) and the mining industry. The farmers' lobby group, the National Farmers' Federation, led by Rick Farley, was, in the end, quite moderate because Farley preached to his constituents that native title was here to stay and that they had to be inside the negotiation process to gain the best outcome.

At the other extreme were a variety of Aboriginal groups who, having at last gained some rights, were not prepared to give them up without a fight, but who did not all agree on what approach to take. Two main groups of Aboriginal negotiators evolved (the so-called A team and B team) pushing slightly different lines – one to the Government and the other to the Greens in the Senate.

The federal Coalition, as Father Frank Brennan pointed

out in his book, *One Land, One Nation*, made things easier in some ways by opting out of the debate – theirs was one less view Keating had to accommodate.[8] The Democrats were basically in agreement with the government, but the Greens wanted to make significant amendments.

Despite all this, eleven months later, after an arduous negotiation process, after months of front-page disclosures about the wrangling and divisions, after the longest Senate debate on record and after 120 amendments had been passed, the *Native Title Act 1993* finally made it through the upper house at almost midnight just three days before Christmas. The politicians and the packed public and press galleries stood and applauded each other.

The Act was the first of the Keating government's three-pronged response to the Mabo decision. It codified the decision of the High Court and set up tribunals and other measures by which native title claims could be mediated, arbitrated and determined.

The second prong was the establishment of a Commonwealth land fund of $1.5 billion over 10 years, which would allow Aboriginal groups who had been dispossessed of their land to buy it back in freehold and maintain it in an attempt to re-establish lost contact with their law and customs.

The third prong was a social justice package to address some of the myriad problems facing that majority of Aborigines who had been irredeemably dispossessed of their land. The social justice package was put on the backburner late in the Keating Government's time in power and is entirely absent from the Howard Government's list of priorities.

The *Native Title Act* was, for indigenous people, the jewel in the crown. It gave Commonwealth statutory authority to Aborigines' claims for vacant Crown land to which they had a connection.

The preamble to the Act defines native title thus: 'The communal, group or individual rights and interests of Aboriginal peoples or Torres Strait Islanders in relation to land or waters where: a) the rights and interests are possessed under the traditional laws acknowledged, and the traditional customs observed, by the Aboriginal people or Torres Strait Islanders; and

b) the Aboriginal peoples or Torres Strait Islanders, by those laws and customs, have a connection with the land or waters; and

c) the rights and interests are recognised by the common law of Australia.'[9]

The Act set up the National Native Title Tribunal, and encouraged the states to set up their own tribunals. It empowered these bodies to receive applications for native title and organise the negotiation and mediation processes by which the applications would be decided. The legislation also laid down the processes by which parties could negotiate and sign their own agreements to recognise native title on parcels of land, or trade title away if they chose.

Problems with the legislation

However, the *Native Title Act* is far from perfect. One seemingly unrelated High Court judgement, the Brandy case, and another in the Federal Court, the Waanyi case, have made the provisions of the Act almost impossible to administer properly.

In *Brandy* a successful constitutional challenge was made in the High Court against the power of tribunals (in this case an anti-discrimination tribunal) to make court-like judgements. This affected the powers of the Native Title Tribunal. In *Waanyi*, another native title case affecting pastoral leases, the Federal Court ruled that the Tribunal had limited power to impose a threshold test to weed out frivolous claims, or claims with little likelihood of success.

The combined result of these two judgements has been that the Tribunal has been forced to accept for mediation every claim put to it except those over freehold land. At the time of writing more than 500 claims were registered, including some multiple claims over single areas of land. Some Aboriginal commentators have said that up to 80 per cent are ambit claims with no possibility of success – a situation that they agree reduces their credibility on other issues.

Meanwhile the state and territory governments have been reluctant to embrace the measures in the Act and slow to set up the machinery to deal with them. In Queensland and Western Australia particularly the governments have tried every method to escape it. So far they have succeeded only in prolonging the argument.

One result is that in some areas development, particularly mining exploration and development in places like Kalgoorlie, has slowed considerably. Another is that farmers who should have no need to fear for their land are faced with native title claims. Another result is that only one mainland determination of title has been ratified (for the Dunghutti people of Crescent Head, NSW, in October 1996). It is not surprising, then, that the chorus of criticism of the Act was loud and increasing, even before the Wik decision was handed down.

Aboriginal negotiators readily concede the Act needs some changing to work effectively. But they also point out that it has been very effective in one way: it has successfully protected their rights from being further eroded.

Some parties have decided that the best way to use the Act is to circumvent its trickiest parts and come to agreements with each other. A land-use agreement was behind the Dunghutti determination. In north Queensland, after two successive state governments delayed the process, mining giant CRA negotiated an agreement with the local Aboriginal claimants, and was given the go-ahead for its massive Century Zinc mine with three months to spare on the time limit. In western South Australia a group of 20 mining exploration companies have signed a model agreement with the legal entity representing Aborigines to smooth negotiations about heritage and native title claims on land earmarked for exploration.

Mining companies have found native title holders willing, if given the chance to negotiate, to allow mining on their land in return for appropriate compensation. This can go beyond cash payments to include jobs packages, sacred sites protection and environmental concessions.

The Cape York Land Use heads of agreement between Aborigines, pastoralists and conservationists was a startling example of what might be possible, and it won moral and financial support from both major parties before the last election (though the Howard and Borbidge Governments' endorsement has waned dramatically since then).

Validation

Perhaps the most controversial (and least understood) part of the *Native Title Act* was the validation of land titles issued after 1975 and before 1994.

Because the High Court said the *Racial Discrimination Act 1975* prevented state governments from legislating to extinguish native title, the Keating Government worried that any leases issued after that date might be invalid. It could have amended the Act, or ridden over it in the *Native Title Act* (because later Commonwealth legislation automatically overrides existing legislation), but the political stigma would have been too great. The Howard Government is aware of the same political danger.

To get around the problem, Keating's advisers wanted to suspend the *Racial Discrimination Act's* operations to make sure grants of title since 1975 were valid. As Frank Brennan pointed out, this suggestion led to allegations of racism and created an emotional breakdown of communications between the Aboriginal negotiators and the Government in October 1993.[10]

The solution, which Brennan described as 'a face-saving device' for all involved, was for the parties to agree that leases issued after 1975 were valid, in return for compensation to Aboriginal groups thus dispossessed, but to call this agreement a 'special measure' under the *Racial Discrimination Act*. The argument was that while in itself the measure was discriminatory, it would combine with the other elements of the Act to be a package of overall benefit to Aboriginal people. If only for political reasons, this measure had to have the agreement of the Aboriginal negotiators, and it was a compromise that the realists on both sides were prepared to make.

So in those final few weeks of negotiations, the 'A-team' of Aboriginal deal-makers agreed that all existing titles could be validated, and agreed to making the *Native Title Act* a special measure under the *Racial Discrimination Act*.

'It's very easy to sort out your common interests'

Ewan Vickery, miners' lawyer, partner, Minter Ellison, Adelaide

'[We recently got together a group of] 14 or 16 mining exploration companies, who all have exploration interests in the far west coastal region of South Australia. There are about 44 mining tenements there within 44,000 square kilometres. There appears to be five distinct Aboriginal groups, and they got coordinated in such a way that it was possible to talk to them through the Aboriginal Legal Rights Movement [ALRM] ...

'In the *Native Title Act*, Section 43 encourages the states and territories to go away and invent their own right to negotiate procedures for mining and exploration. And South Australia is the only state that's done it so far ... it's called Part 9B of the *Mining Act* ... In South Australia you are granted your tenement but you can't exercise its privileges if you might affect native title ... If you're in native title risk country you have to go and get a court determination or an agreement. Now we all know a court determination is going to take *n* years, and it will probably cost you between two and five million dollars, because the level of evidence that needs to be established is just huge ... It's a can of worms.

'So we finished up with a mediation on 1 and 2 April brought on by the Native Title Tribunal trying to get through its list. They brought it on because the Aboriginal groups seemed to be able to hold their working group together, and it seemed to have a chance because these working groups notoriously get formed one day and break down the next – that's just Aboriginal politics still trying to adjust, I think.

'What [the Aborigines'] lawyers were saying was, "Look, to attract you guys over to the west of Gawler Craton, what about we say you come on, do your exploration, we come to some arrangement about getting it checked out by an anthropologist or two for heritage matters, and we won't ask you for any money, you just pick up the cost of the anthropologist."

'We're thinking, "Well, that's just in conformity with our *Aboriginal Heritage Act* in South Australia" ... So we decided to tell the mediator ... "We think there's a chance ..."

'[The Aborigines' lawyer] Darcy O'Shea consulted with the legal rights movement people and put together a little agreement as a draft, and I then convened a meeting of the exploration companies and chamber of mines officers ... You're going to be talking to substantially the same people for both heritage and native title, therefore you only want to come to one arrangement, not two. It's like having two contracts to buy a car. So I welded together the contractual principles to deal with both. And we called this "The Model Agreement" ...

'At least initially, until there's a bit more experience, most companies are just saying "Yes, that's fine" and there's nothing to change from the model – all you do is add your mining interests, and there's also a process for working out a budget ...

'What would I say to other people around the country? Well, it depends. I've had clients from Western Australia quite upset that they've had to put cash in [Aboriginal] negotiators' hands if they want something signed. And they find that repulsive. But they are being told that some companies are doing that, if you don't do it you don't get yours signed. Now, that's blackmail. We've had attempts to do it here – but this group has vowed to resist it. We will work through the working group ...

'Even in South Australia all I can say is, "Part 9B really does funnel you towards a personal negotiated agreement rather than a litigious outcome, for reasons of timing and cost, and, in the business you are in, there really isn't an alternative to agreement" ...

Where you can build relationships it's very easy to sort out your common interests, and come to mutually acceptable arrangements. But getting there is the big difficulty, because most Aboriginal groups are not cohesive.'

The right to negotiate

One of the possibilities discussed in the early negotiations for the legislation was that Aborigines be able to veto mining activity on their land. It was a right they were given under the *Northern Territory Land Rights Act* in 1976, and one they wanted again. But Keating would not agree. The Aborigines were, in the end, forced to give it up, but they exacted a price: the right to negotiate.

This right was included as part of the *Native Title Act*, and as a special measure under the *Racial Discrimination Act*, because Aboriginal groups see their traditional law (which led to the Mabo decision in the first place) as conferring on them the right to have a say in the way their land is used by a third party. The *Native Title Act* establishes a mechanism whereby if a government wants to issue a title over a piece of land to a third party, or the right to use the land for a particular purpose, any Aboriginal claimant of that land has the ability to negotiate terms for six months before other elements of the Act come into play.

If, for example, the Western Australian government wants to allow mining on a piece of land, or a mining company to explore that piece of land, the Aboriginal inhabitants can require the company to negotiate with them if the action threatens their enjoyment of their native title. The condition is that they must be registered with the Native Title Tribunal as a claimant before being granted the right to negotiate. After the six-month negotiation process is complete, and if no agreement has been reached, the claim can be arbitrated by the tribunal, or a government minister can override the claim if he or she thinks it is in the national or state interest to do so.

This right to negotiate was considered one of the key elements of the *Native Title Act*. The preamble to the Act says: 'In future, acts that affect native title should only be able to be validly done if, typically, they can also be done to freehold land and if, whenever appropriate, every reasonable effort has been made to secure the agreement of the native title holders through a special right to negotiate'.[11]

It is one of the most significant rights Aborigines have won from the whole native title debate. But, as explained in

Chapter 3, the Howard Government opposes this right for a variety of reasons, and has shown a clear intention to water it down. In some cases it would be removed entirely.

The vexed question of leases

Both the Mabo decision and the subsequent legislation left the legal position of leasehold title as a mystery. The question of two leases granted on areas of the Murray Islands came up in the Mabo case. One was granted in 1882 to the London Missionary Society, and another, a 20-year lease issued in 1931 over two whole islands, Dauar and Waier, to two non-islanders, for the purposes of building a sardine factory.

The Court in 1992 was split on the significance of these grants. The sardine factory lease had certain conditions, including that the lessees 'shall not in any way obstruct or interfere with the use by the Murray Island natives of their tribunal [tribal] gardens and plantation of the leased land'. A similar condition was attached to prevent the leaseholders interfering with traditional fishing rights on the island's reefs.[12]

Justice Brennan, whose judgement was the most influential of the Court's pronouncements in *Mabo*, thought that on both those leases, conditions notwithstanding, native title had been extinguished. 'By granting the lease, the Crown purported to confer possessory rights on the lessee and to acquire for itself the reversion expectant on the termination of the lease. The sum of those rights would have left no room for the continued existence of rights and interests derived from Meriam Laws and customs,' he wrote.[13]

But Justices William Deane (now the Governor-General), Mary Gaudron and John Toohey disagreed. Deane and Gaudron said in their joint judgement that none of the grants 'had the effect of extinguishing the existing rights of Murray Islanders under common law native title'. The reservation clauses, they said, 'should clearly be construed as intended to protect, rather than extinguish, any existing native rights of occupation and use,' and therefore 'common law native title of Murray Islanders ... survives'.[14]

Not having heard detailed argument on these questions, the Court decided to leave a pronouncement on the lease issue until a later time. Its orders specifically left out the islands of Dauer and Waier and the board of missions land.

But while the specific instances involved in the Murray Island leases were small, they had much wider ramifications. It was not that missions and sardine factories were particularly significant on their own in the history of Australian land tenure, but that the way in which they were legally set up was of crucial significance. The question of the issue of leases and the conditions (or reservations) on their use by Aborigines has direct ramifications for one of the most widespread forms of land management in Australia's rural and remote areas – pastoral leases.

While the Mabo decision dealt with unalienated (vacant) Crown land, such areas make up a comparatively small proportion of the country, and they are, almost by definition, lands that nobody, with the exception of the Aboriginal owners, is very interested in. Pastoral leases, on the other hand, take up a huge proportion of the country and well-heeled white landowners are extremely interested in them.

Ticking away inside the Mabo judgement was a time bomb. From the moment it was handed down, and the moment legislation was framed to reflect it, pastoral leases were destined to be the next major battleground where the rules governing native title would be fought out.

What is a pastoral lease?

The squatters

The nineteenth century Australian habit of squatting has had mixed public relations over the years.

To governments of the time, the first squatters were considered pesky, greedy, unable to be regulated – they were getting something for nothing. But as they started producing the beef and mutton that provided the growing colony with some of the comforts of home, this attitude quickly swung around. They became seen as Australia's version of the frontiersmen – pioneers, hardy types who were willing to brave danger, drought and isolation to cut civilisation out of bushland.

Later, as the fruits of these endeavours began to flow to

their descendants, the top rung of squatters became part of the establishment. The *Macquarie Dictionary* lists one definition of 'squatter' as being 'one of a group of rich and influential rural landowners'.

But as the unauthorised movement of settlers and stock into the so-called waste-lands accelerated in the middle part of last century, the government devised a system of pastoral leases and licences in an attempt to regulate the holdings and activities of the squatters. The first of these pieces of legislation, passed in New South Wales in 1839, was the *Crown Lands unauthorized Occupation Act*. This set up a system of occupation licences, under which a fee was payable for an annual licence to occupy Crown lands. The Act also set up a border police force to control and protect the activities of the pioneers.

In 1842, with the *Sale of Waste Lands Act*, the New South Wales government brought the management of 'waste' country into the land tenure system for the first time. In 1846 that Act was amended allowing the government from the following year to issue leases of up to 14 years' duration.

While these pastoral leases were based on long-established land management principles, they were, of necessity, reinvented to fit the Australian context. According to Justice Toohey in his Wik judgement, the 1846 Act was the first step towards the invention of what became a 'multitude of Australian tenures of new types'.[15]

When Queensland was divided from New South Wales and made a separate colony in 1859, the established laws, including those governing land tenure, were transferred to the northern jurisdiction. Between 1860 and 1862 the Queensland legislature made scores of different laws to govern the leasing and use of the vast tracts of countryside available for grazing cattle and sheep. These laws were related to each other, and to the British system of land tenure, but were adapted to fit the unique conditions of Australia's vast hinterland.

A. C. and G. W. Millard wrote in *The Law of Real Property in NSW* in 1905 of the 'numerous and elaborate provisions' governing the occupation of Crown land in Australia: 'Nothing corresponding to the body of laws thereby created is found in English law, there being nothing in England analogous to the vast area of unoccupied lands in this colony, of which the Crown is the nominal, and the public the real owner, the settlement of which is necessary to the welfare and progress of the country.'[16]

The Wik case looked specifically at the situation in Queensland, but the spread of pastoral leaseholdings had occurred in every state all over the continent. The result of these laws is astounding: pastoral leases now cover 42 per cent of the entire continent. In some states (South Australia, Queensland, the Northern Territory and Western Australia) they cover up to 70 per cent of the land area. Some of the individual leases also cover unimaginably huge areas – larger than some European countries. Many, because of their poor quality, are used at an extremely low intensity, attract very low per-hectare rents, and are rarely, if ever, occupied by white people.

Conditions on leases

The leasehold system worked well for the new colony. It became so widespread because it had so many advantages in the push to cultivate the land. The squatters gained access to tracts of land at rates they could afford. For the colonial administrators, apart from legitimising and regulating the activities of the squatters, it had the virtue of spurring on the economy and giving the treasury some regular revenue from the payment of licence fees. In addition leasehold allowed the Crown to make useful the vast rangelands of Australia over which it had radical title, without actually selling them to the squatters and losing any future rights over them.

Justice Toohey wrote that the complicated lease and licence regime 'reflects the desire of pastoralists for some form of security of title and the clear intention of the Crown that the pastoralists should not acquire the freehold of large areas of land, the future use of which could not be readily foreseen.'[17]

It was presumably because governments did not want to permanently lose control over these huge areas that they attached so many conditions to the use of pastoral leaseholdings. For example, most of these leases were described in their terms and conditions as being 'for pastoral purposes only',[18] effectively ruling out any activity except the grazing of livestock and the building of whatever structures were required to facilitate this (fences, mustering yards, stables or machinery sheds and, later, airstrips).

But governments took the opportunities presented by leases to attach much more onerous conditions, too. On one of the Queensland holdings under examination in the Wik case (see p. 43), the lease stipulated that the pastoralists allow on the property any authorised person to explore or work the land for gold or other minerals, and to remove timber, stone, gravel, clay or guano. The lessee was prevented from ringbarking, cutting or destroying trees, but could not restrict other authorised people from removing timber or other material. Drovers could even pasture stock if a stock route passed through the property. Furthermore, the leaseholder was required to allow authorised people 'at all times to go upon the said Land, or any part thereof, for any purpose whatsoever, or to make any survey, inspection, or examination of the same'.[19]

Similar conditions were placed on leases around the country, and none of these so-called reservations interfered with the prime purpose of the squatters: raising cattle, rounding them up and selling them.

Pastoralists now argue that their interests have expanded enormously since these leases were granted. Irrigation and cropping, though not conferred as statutory rights in the leases, are common practices now, and have been encouraged by governments to enhance the value of the rangelands. Burning and clearing and the control of rabbits and other vermin have also been widely practised, although they are not specifically allowed by their leases.

Protection of Aborigines

The history of the leasehold system also tells of another reason that land was made leasehold rather than freehold – the protection of the Aboriginal inhabitants from the excesses of the squatters.

According to New South Wales Governor Sir George Gipps in a letter to the British Secretary of State, Lord

Glenelg, in the early 19th Century, the *Crown Lands unau-thorized Occupation Act* was enacted partly 'for the purpose of putting a stop to the atrocities which have been committed both on them [the natives] and by them'. A licence could be cancelled if the licensee was convicted 'of any malicious injury committed upon or against any aboriginal native or other persons,' Gipps wrote.[20]

Another Secretary of State, Earl Grey, seemed particularly anxious to ensure the rights of the Aboriginal people on the Australian rangelands, writing many missives on the subject. In 1849 he wrote to Governor Sir Charles FitzRoy that the pastoral runs were designed to give rights to pasture only, 'not the exclusive occupation of the Land, as against Natives using it for the ordinary purposes'.[21]

It was obvious, however, that these sanctions did not always translate to the Australian bush. They certainly did not stop the settlers from persecuting the indigenous population. The settlement of some of the remote regions of the country was characterised by the slaughter and dispossession of the native populations, and some violence against isolated white settlers in return.

The Northern Protector of Aboriginals, Walter Roth, said in his 1900 annual report that, 'It would be as well, I think, to point out to certain of these Northern cattle-men (at all events those few amongst them who regard the natives as nothing more than vermin, worthy only of being trampled on) that their legal status on the lands they thus rent amounts only to this: There is nothing illegal in either blacks (or Europeans) travelling through unfenced lease-hold runs. These runs are held only on grazing rights – the right to the grass – and can only be upheld as against people taking stock, etc., through them'.[22]

These sorts of concerns were replicated around the country in the 19th and early 20th centuries by protectors of Aborigines and others. Very early precedents show that land was leased to squatters rather than sold to them partly in an attempt to end the violence against Aborigines and to encourage an early form of coexistence.

In the states in the western part of the country, this system was much more clearly codified, and exists to the present. In the Northern Territory the land legislation allowed Aborigines free access to pastoral leases as well as the right to take and kill native animals for food or ceremonial purposes, take water, conduct ceremonies and use any plant growing naturally on the land. In South Australia the leases allowed Aborigines not only to take food but also to erect dwellings. In Western Australia anybody could wander on pastoral land (as long as it was not enclosed or improved), and Aborigines were additionally permitted to hunt and gather food.[23] (In a travesty of that legislation, in Western Australia some pastoralists erect fences with locked gates to keep Aborigines living in small patches of their country, unable to get access to the rest.)

It is clear from these statutory conditions that pastoral leases of this nature should not be confused with farms cleared and used for cropping. The High Court found that no government had ever intended that pastoral leases mimic freehold ownership of land. The history of pastoral leases indicates that they were invented to allow the use of land for particular purposes and for limited (albeit long) periods. While in some cases the provisions designed for the protection of Aboriginal inhabitants were not adhered to, in many cases they were.

Apart from the mention of Aborigines in the reservations to the lease legislation in the three western states, indigenous people were rarely, if ever, mentioned in land Acts. This did not imply that they were to be regarded as trespassers – in fact, precisely the opposite. Their continued presence on leasehold land in the remoter parts of Australia seems to have been taken for granted.

'They are a displaced race'

Joy Marriott, pastoralist, Queensland, Mountain View, Lakeland

' … I grew up at a place called Line Hill, which is on the coast next to what is now the Lockhart River. My parents owned it for quite a while, and if there's anyone up here who has a reason to have an attitude against Aborigines, it's me. In 1972 the National Party excised half the property and gave it to the Aborigines, and they set up the Lockhart community on it. My parents sold the property a year later and moved out west.

'But while we had that property we used to go to Coen, where there was the Australian Inland Mission. It was a hostel ... and we went to school with the local Aborigines. Coen keeps coming back into it actually – it was at Coen in August 1995 we [the Peninsula branch of the Cattlemen's Union] had a meeting and agreed to the first resolution for coexistence [with Aborigines].

'Anyway my parents had left the peninsula and I came up to work on properties under the Brucellosis and Tuberculosis Eradication Scheme. I worked with a lot of Aboriginal stockmen, and got to have an even better knowledge of them.

'Then I married Peter Marriott, who was managing Crocodile and Holroyd, in 1986. Crocodile was 600 square miles and ... it was owned by some city doctors. They gave back 400 square miles to the local Aborigines and that became Quinkan reserve, where they have the Laura Dance Festival, and where the cave paintings are ... It didn't affect the viability or saleability of the place. We sold it for $1.8 million and the fellow we sold it to sold it again for more. And now there are no native title claims because the Aborigines have got what they wanted, they had no need to acquire what was left ...

'I understand the fear [of other pastoralists], but I don't think by people taking too extreme a view that we are going to solve anything. My belief is before the native title claims started, we had everything to lose and nothing to gain, but the Aboriginal people had nothing to lose and everything to gain, because they started off with nothing – we had taken it all from them ... We were going to lose something, and we're better off to volunteer what to lose instead of having it being made statutory and forcing us.

'I believe they had a big injustice done to them and they are a displaced race. Growing up here I understand their connection to place, because I have a connection too. But also they've got their special Dreamtime connection. It is real to them, so it is not up to us to tell them what that is ...

'Rather than wear what happens right at the end, I would rather we go on the front foot and have a say.'

Coexistence and the cattle industry

As a result of these rules and reservations, many pastoralists, particularly in the remote regions of the country, have always lived in coexistence with Aboriginal people on the same land.

On much of this land coexistence was far from a burden to the pastoralists. Apart from the early human rights considerations of allowing Aborigines to live on and use their land, the reservation rules proved very beneficial for pastoralists over many years, because they soon realised that the local indigenous people were a plentiful source of cheap labour for the cattle runs. The more remote the run, the more difficult (and expensive) it was to secure the services of white labour, so Aborigines were trained in horsemanship and turned into stockmen.

In some ways they were uniquely suited to the work. They knew the country well enough to find cattle for the muster, they knew how to find water and food for themselves and the livestock in the driest times, and they were very unlikely to get lost on their own land. The National Indigenous Working Group on Native Title, set up to negotiate with the Commonwealth Government about the Wik judgement, has described the Aboriginal stockmen as the 'backbone of the pastoral industry'. Without their labour some more marginal enterprises would not have been viable.[24]

But the indigenous stockmen were rarely paid except in rations, and whatever pay they did receive was nowhere near the award rate for white stockmen. Thus (in a bitter irony) the otherwise enlightened Federal Government decision in 1968 to force pastoralists to pay Aboriginal stockmen the standard rate had the unintended consequence that they were sacked wholesale and many forced away from their traditional lands – some for the first time since white colonisation.

Pastoral leases and native title

The question before the High Court in the Wik case was quite simple. The Court had already found in *Mabo* that the Crown's assumption of radical title had not by itself extinguished native title. Now it was being asked if the granting of pastoral leases had done so.

Most commentators thought they had. Brennan's Mabo judgement seemed to be quite clear on this point. He wrote that: 'If a lease be granted, the lessee acquires possession [of the land] and the Crown acquires the reversion expectant on the expiry of the term'.[25] Deane and Gaudron disagreed in the case of the sardine factory and the mission lease, but wrote nonetheless that: 'The personal rights conferred by common law native title do not constitute an estate or interest in the land itself. They are extinguished by an unqualified grant of an inconsistent estate in the land by the Crown, such as a grant in fee or a lease conferring the right to exclusive possession.'[26]

On the basis of those indications, the government wrote into the preamble to the *Native Title Act* that the High Court had 'held that native title is extinguished by valid government acts that are inconsistent with the continued existence of native title rights and interests, such as the grant of freehold or leasehold estates'.[27] However, the phrase in the preamble to the Act was repeated nowhere in the actual provisions of the Act because it was too contentious an issue to be resolved by the legislation. The Government had legal advice that if it legislated to extinguish title on pastoral leases and this was subsequently found by the High Court to be an invalid action, the Commonwealth might be liable for billions of dollars in compensation.

Certainly the Aboriginal negotiators hammering out a deal with Keating in 1993 never accepted that they had to give up any claim to pastoral leases. It would take another High Court judgement to clarify the issue.

When the Wik case finally came before it in 1996, the Court was acutely aware of the importance of its decision. Not only were vast sections of Australia's land mass at stake, but so, perhaps, were the holdings of some of the biggest names in Australia, and one of the country's largest industries. A proportion of pastoral land is run by family farmers, and in some states land is reserved for family holdings. But large companies, like AMP, and hugely rich individuals, such as Rupert Murdoch, Kerry Packer and Janet Holmes a Court, are also big leaseholders. Packer owns 37 per cent of the pastoral land in the Kimberley region. A cousin of senior Federal Government minister Ian McLachlan is Australia's top private landholder (a list of large landholders is attached, Appendix 2). The cattle barons wield enormous political and financial power and their produce earns Australia billions of export dollars.

However, as Justice Kirby recognised in his Wik judgement, the issues were also of crucial importance to Aborigines. If the High Court found that pastoral leases extinguished native title, the Mabo decision would be 'revealed as having little practical significance' for the majority of Australia's indigenous people. Kirby wrote:

> The vulnerability of native title to extinguishment by the fact or necessary incidents of a grant of a pastoral lease over the land is revealed in sharp relief. The effective operation of the *Native Title Act 1993* ... as well as claims under the general law, recede to apply only to the balance of Australia's land surface after the grants of estates, including freehold and pastoral leaseholds ... are deducted. This is all the more significant to indigenous peoples as the parts of Australia where their laws and traditions (important to sustain native title) are most likely to have survived include those where pastoral leases are likely to exist.[28]

The other group which stood to gain or lose from the issue were the politicians. Keating's habit of elevating native title (and his role in it) to the centre of political debate meant the spotlight would be once again on the High Court in the leadup to the Wik decision. Even before the Court made its judgement, the politicians were hard at work speculating about the outcome. The 1996 election, when John Howard was seeking to take government after 13 years of Labor rule, only served to intensify their gaze.

What was the Coalition's position on native title before the Wik decision?

'Say as little as possible'

The Coalition's 1996 election policy document on native title was very brief and somewhat vague.

After criticising the Keating government's legislation, and promising to increase its 'workability,' the document addressed the pastoral lease problem in these terms: 'The issue of whether pastoral leases extinguish native title remains before the courts. So long as this issue remains undecided, there will be uncertainty for indigenous people and potential developers, and hardship within the pastoral industry. A Coalition government will undertake extensive consultations with all stakeholders to see early resolution of these uncertainties.'[29]

The policy document went on to say that it would respect the fact of native title, the right to compensation for those whose property was resumed, the 'special relationship' between Aborigines and land and, crucially, 'the prohibition of racially discriminatory measures or laws'.[30]

With the possible exception of the latter provision, it was a document designed, as all such things are in modern politics, to say as little as possible.

A pastoralist from the Coalition's core bush constituency who saw the promise to act decisively on the pastoral lease issue might have looked forward to legislation extinguishing title on those leases. On the other hand, a swinging city voter concerned about Aboriginal rights in general, would have noted the promise not to act in a racially discriminatory way. In the atmosphere of the election campaign (in which Bob Katter and Pauline Hanson were making the race debate a problem for the Coalition) it was a policy with something for everyone. In other words it was typical of most of the Coalition's policies in the leadup to the 1996 election – safe, bland, and inoffensive.

But after the election was won the rhetoric of 'workability' had to be followed through with policy, and that required some tough choices.

The Coalition had foundered on Aboriginal affairs before. John Hewson committed one of his worst in a long line of political blunders in 1993 by refusing to support any part of the *Native Title Act*, even those amendments supported by the miners and farmers, because he did not want any role in its passage. This refusal made sure of two things only – firstly that some National Party senators would cross the floor to get some industry-sponsored amendments through, and secondly that his party would be completely marginalised in the debate.

Alexander Downer also had his problems. His trip to central Australia during his short leadership of the party in 1994 was one of the defining moments of his downfall. He proved on that trip that he had no knowledge or understanding of native title, no plan for how to deal with it and only very limited ability to think on his feet.

Howard's problems with Aboriginal affairs started from the first days of his Prime Ministership. Accountability in ATSIC was the subject of his first Cabinet meeting and his first Canberra press conference. In those early days, Howard, his Aboriginal Affairs Minister, John Herron, and a tough-talking Cabinet conspired to attack ATSIC to the extent that the Aboriginal leadership believed their worst fears were being realised. It was not long before the Social Justice Commissioner, Mick Dodson, announced a crisis in relations between Aborigines and the government over a whole range of issues.

It was in this atmosphere of suspicion that Aborigines approached negotiations with the government about its planned amendments to the *Native Title Act*.

Backbench revolt

The man in charge of the government's consultations on native title was Senator Nick Minchin, one of Howard's most trusted lieutenants. Minchin, a conservative South Australian, became Howard's parliamentary secretary for native title and constitutional change. He is politically astute and an extremely good tactician who travelled with Howard for much of the election campaign to help deal with problems which arose along the way. But in dealing with this most thorny of issues, Minchin had problems of his own. After a two-month tour of Australia consulting with the parties, he came up with an outline of his proposed amendment, called *Towards a More Workable Native Title Act*. Cabinet considered and approved the discussion document on 6 May, but three days later the backbench revolted, with up to a third of Howard's party room demanding he and Minchin change their approach.

The catalyst? Cabinet's choice to leave up to the High Court the decision about whether pastoral leases extinguished native title. 'It would be an understatement for me to say I would be devastated to learn I am now part of a governing party that so lacks the commitment and intestinal fortitude that it is prepared to abdicate its legislative responsibility to our Courts,' wrote WA backbencher Wilson Tuckey to his leader John Howard on the following day.[31]

Two weeks later, after making some concessions to the demands from the backbench, Minchin and Howard finally released the discussion paper to the public.

Amendments to the *Native Title Act*

It was no surprise that the Government's position on pastoral leases was the same as it had always been – to extinguish title on leases would breach the *Racial Discrimination Act* (in contravention of its election commitment). Extinguishment would also involve acquiring property and providing compensation, estimated at up to billions of dollars. The discussion paper pointed out that 'The ensuing litigation would pre-empt the certainty sought by the proponents of the legislative extinguishment option, possibly for a long period.'[32]

The position, in a nutshell, was to let the High Court decide, and to abide by that decision.

However, the paper did propose significant expansion of the activities that could be conducted on pastoral leases. Where most leases allowed the pastoralist to do nothing but graze livestock, this paper proposed allowing agricultural, commercial or tourism activities on the land 'without changing the character of the lease as pastoral'. Aboriginal groups argued that some of these provisions would, in themselves, be inconsistent with native title. They also warned that, if any of these activities extinguished title, the relevant government would be liable for compensation. Aboriginal negotiator Noel Pearson said at a press conference in Canberra in mid-1996 that the proposals represented 'extinguishment by stealth'.

The Minchin paper was very tough on indigenous people in other respects too, proposing the substantial winding back of Aboriginal rights under the *Native Title Act*. One of the key proposals reduced the access of native title claimants to the right to negotiate. Aborigines would be prevented from negotiating at the exploration stage of mining, where before they could negotiate both at the exploration and development stages. No renewal of a mining lease would be subject to negotiation. As a sop to the extinguishment-mad backbench the government also promised to consider allowing only those Aborigines whose right to native title had been actually proven (rather than just claimed) to have access to the right to negotiate. Considering that by this point no native title claim except that of Eddie Mabo's Meriam people had resulted in a determination of title, this would have been a very tough test.

Aboriginal groups, led by Social Justice Commissioner Mick Dodson, said these provisions would breach the spirit of the *Native Title Act*, and therefore breach the *Racial Discrimination Act*. Any such breach would break a Coalition election promise. Dodson said the changes went against the spirit of the special measure negotiated with Keating under the race Act.

To overcome the difficulties encountered since the Waanyi case, the Minchin paper also proposed making it more difficult for native title claimants to gain access to the native title tribunal's processes. The toughened threshold test involved claimants making a detailed application for title and having that application endorsed by the local Aboriginal representative body. Only if the tribunal found prima facie evidence that the claim could be sustained would the claimants get access to the tribunal's processes.

Other provisions would have allowed:

- the federal minister to override a claim made in the national interest *before* any negotiation of the claim had taken place (this would mainly have affected claims over mining leases);
- shortened time-frames for mediation and arbitration;
- more funding for Aboriginal representative bodies, and much more onerous accountability requirements;
- more scope for land use agreements between parties;
- provision for such agreements to include a share of the profits of a development.

The consensus among Aboriginal leaders was that almost every provision in this discussion paper was adverse to the interests of native title holders. In a press release of 23 May, the then head of the Aboriginal and Torres Strait Islander Commission, Lois O'Donoghue, said the paper had been the result of an unsatisfactory consultation process and represented an 'unseemly scramble' by the government to amend the *Native Title Act* and bring about a 'significant diminution of the rights of native title holders'.

The Government introduced the amendments in the House of Representatives in June. In October it introduced further amendments to the Bill which, among other things, removed the concession to its backbench, saying claimants of native title, not just those who had proved their title, would still have access to the right to negotiate.[33]

But the amendments to the amendments also removed the provision allowing Aborigines to share in the profits of a development on their land, and said that interference in the spiritual life of a community should be removed from the list of activities that triggered the right to negotiate.

Those amendments are included in the huge set of changes tabled in the wake of the Wik decision.

Pressure on Howard

This is the context into which the Wik decision dropped. Months before the High Court delivered its judgement, the stage was set for a confrontation between the Government, its suspicious back bench, the conservative state governments, and the Aboriginal negotiators, who had been made acutely aware that there was a new power in town.

The pressures John Howard has been under since the Wik decision are not new – he has been facing them since early 1996. They were the same pressures Paul Keating faced in 1993, but they are perhaps even more intense for a conservative leader with a large and frightened rural constituency.

The sheer size of the areas of land involved in pastoral leases and the economic imperative for securing development gave rural backbenchers, farmers, miners and premiers strong reasons to put pressure on John Howard and Nick Minchin to legislate to extinguish native title on pastoral leases. But legislating to extinguish was something the government refused to do. Why should they wear the political stigma (and compensation cost) of doing such a thing when their legal advice was confident that the High Court would do the job for them?

Their argument, right up until the Wik decision was announced on 23 December 1996, was that the High Court should be allowed to decide the issue, and that its decision should stand. But what the High Court actually did was to vindicate the position of the Aborigines, and justify the worst nightmares of all the other powerful groups.

Far from relieving the government of the pressure to extinguish by legislation, the High Court had redoubled it.

2

The Wik Decision

What was the Wik case about?

Stark facts

In the middle of 1993, as the Keating Government was still tussling with its constituencies and its conscience about how to best put the results of the Mabo decision into legislation, another group of Aborigines was taking direct action and applying to the Federal Court to have its native title recognised.

The Wik peoples live, as they have always done, north of the Edward River and east towards Coen on the Cape York peninsula in far north Queensland. The land they sought to have recognised as theirs was mostly part of the Holroyd River holding – a huge pastoral lease 2830 km^2 (1119 square miles) in area.

A neighbouring group of Aborigines, the Thayorre people, later also claimed a section of land which bordered and partly overlapped the southern portion of the Wik claim, around the Edward River. The major portion of their claim was for an area of land that had once been part of the Mitchellton pastoral lease, and was 1385 km^2 (535 square miles) in area. Because the two claims overlapped, the court decided to hear them as part of the same legal action before the Federal Court, and later the High Court.[1]

The history of these two holdings shows clearly that

pastoral leases in such remote areas are nothing like the family farms in other more densely populated parts of Australia. The facts in this case were so stark they were quoted at length by most of the judges in their High Court decisions. They throw into clear relief the moral questions at stake and show exactly why the judges dashed the expectations of most of the Australian establishment in such dramatic fashion by ruling that native title could survive on pastoral leaseholdings.

The Thayorre claim: the Mitchellton lease

Part of the Mitchellton land, which made up most of the Thayorre claim, had first been opened for pastoral development by the government of Queensland in 1912, under the *Land Act* which had been gazetted two years earlier. It granted an occupation licence to a settler called William Hutson for an area of about 100 square miles (260km^2). That licence was to last until the end of that year and thereafter from year to year as long as the rent was paid. Hutson failed to pay the rent at all and so forfeited the licence. In 1915, the Government tried again, notifying potential pioneers that the whole area was now open for settlement. A grazier could have a pastoral lease with a tenure of up to 30 years.[2]

Three men applied for and were granted use of the land until 1930, but they forfeited that right just three years later, also by failing to pay the rent. The courts were satisfied that, like Hutson, those lessees had never actually taken possession of the land.[3]

In 1918 the Government tried yet again, and Walter Hood was granted the use of the land for 30 years. A few months later he transferred his interest to a company, Byrimine Pastoral Properties Limited, but it too held the land for only three years before surrendering it in 1921 without ever taking possession.[4]

At that point there was a suggestion that the company would surrender the lease, and the Chief Protector of Aboriginals, Walter Roth, wrote to the government to point out there were 'about 300 natives roaming on [the] country'. He argued that if the company allowed its lease to lapse, his department should be informed before another lease was issued, presumably so he could have a say in how the new lessee should act to protect the rights of the indigenous inhabitants.[5]

In January 1922 the Mitchellton land was temporarily reserved for the use of Aborigines. In May 1930, it was permanently reserved for that purpose. Part of that land is now held in trust by the Pormpuraaw Aboriginal Council.[6]

None of the leases issued by the Queensland government over the Mitchellton land contained an explicit guarantee that the pastoralist would have exclusive possession of the land. In fact, there were conditions ('reservations') which restricted the use of the land by the pastoralist, and also specifically allowed the government to authorise other activities on it.

As noted earlier, the most important condition was that the lease was for 'pastoral purposes only'; that is, it could be used only to graze cattle or other stock. Other conditions were that the pastoralists would allow anybody authorised by the government to search for or work the land for gold or other minerals or to remove timber, stone, gravel, clay or guano. The lessee was prevented from ringbarking, cutting or destroying trees and could not restrict other authorised people from removing timber or other material. Others could pasture stock if a stock route passed through.[7]

The leaseholder, in the words of the lease, was to allow authorised people 'at all times to go upon the said Land, or any part thereof, for any purpose whatsoever, or to make any survey, inspection, or examination of the same'. The second Mitchellton lease also specifically allowed exploration for petrol.[8]

In addition, the High Court judges found that, while the leaseholders had the right to ban trespassers, Aborigines had never been considered to be trespassers. The various reports from the protectors of Aborigines throughout the nineteenth century showed that Aborigines continued to live, apparently rarely disturbed, on the lands.

In some other jurisdictions (Western Australia, Northern Territory and South Australia) entreaties from the colonial masters in England that Aborigines not be hunted off their lands had led to specific clauses in all pastoral leases (also called reservations) which allowed Aboriginal people to live their lives in their accustomed manner. Those reservations exist in those states' statutes to this day.

These various conditions imposed on the leaseholders were to play a crucial role in the legal arguments presented to the High Court, and in the final decision the Court made.

'We are here too'

Francis Yunkaporta, Wik elder, Aurukun, Queensland

'I'm involved in the Wik case … I'm on the Aurukun reserve and before that the mission used to be managing it. Then after a while, when we had a smash-up fight with the state government, then we changed and became a local government.

'So we are still the Aurukun people. We've been here for a long time. We were brought in here from north, south, east and west, each area not far from Aurukun. So we are still Aurukun people because we are on Aurukun reserve.

'I wasn't [in Canberra when the decision was handed down] but we came afterwards over to Canberra. We went in afterwards and we had a talk with the Prime Minister and asked him about if we can have the land given back to us, you know, ownership of the lands, so that we are able to be aware of the land, and owner of the land, like it used to be in the time when our ancestors used to live.

'I think the Prime Minister is not taking any notice. You know we told him that we have a custom, we have a culture, customary law, and we also speak your language as well. But I think that he is not really listening to Aurukun people, and is not aware of, does not recognise Aboriginal people. The way he speaks. I mean, he don't care …

'I mean the court recognised we are the Aboriginal people. The land that we are living on around this area, we belong to the land. I think, for instance, Mabo, he was connected to the Torres Strait Island, but we fought it before Mabo. And our Wik decision, the court made it clear that the land belonged to the Aboriginal people. We feel proud that the court made that decision because we are Aboriginal people.

'The Prime Minister – the way he speaks – we have tried to talk to him when we were down in Canberra. We won the Wik case, but the Prime Minister argues about this native title, he's aware of that. But we are not trying to get the land from the farmers. They've got their businesses. All that we're really talking about is the land that we are trying to protect. They've got cattle, they've got people on farms, well, that was taken from the people, but we're not talking about those, because they've got a business to do. But if they are able to negotiate with the people, and we can also negotiate with them – we are here too, but they realise that, you know, what they did was the wrong thing.'

The Wik claim: the Holroyd River holding
The Holroyd River holding, which largely made up the land the Wik people were claiming, was more than twice the area of the Mitchellton at 1119 square miles (2830 km²).

The Queensland government did not declare this parcel of land open to be leased until June 1944. In February 1945 it was granted for 30 years and was transferred a number of times, but, unlike Mitchellton, the leaseholders actually took up the lease and ran cattle on the land. In 1972 the then leaseholder successfully applied for a new lease, which was granted for 30 years from 1 January 1974. In 1986 the *Land Act* was amended, and under the provisions of that amendment, the term of the lease was extended for another 20 years.[9]

In 1972, 27 years after the lease was first issued, the Holroyd land was described by the lessees as having natural water only, bloodwood, ironwood, stringy bark, ti-tree, messmate (a kind of gum tree), ironstone ridges with some melon holes (shallow water holes), and some spear grass. It was country that was suitable purely for breeding cattle, not for fattening them. It was able to handle about one beast on every 25 hectares (60 acres) in open range conditions, and had no improvements and no accommodation.[10]

Like the Mitchellton lease, several conditions were required of the leaseholder as part of the 1974 Holroyd River lease, but they were much more detailed and onerous. The government stipulated that within five years the leaseholders must: construct 'to the satisfaction of the Minister' a manager's residence, quarters for five men, a machinery shed, an airstrip to the standard expected by the Department of Civil Aviation to accept mail and flying doctor services, a set of main yards, a dip and three earth dams; erect 145 km of internal fencing; sow at least 40.5 hectares as a seed production area and enclose the whole lot with a 'good and substantial fence'.[11] The leaseholders were further required to maintain all these improvements in good and working order.

Most of these conditions were broken. An inspection report in 1984 revealed that 10 years later an airstrip had been built, but none of the buildings had been constructed. There was no plan for a seed production area. No boundary fencing had been erected and none was intended. About 1000 head of cattle were on the property and it was characterised as being 'not permanently occupied'.[12]

Employees were as few and far between as the cattle, the report noting, 'No one [was] employed at the time of inspection though usually about 12 stockmen are mustering the block in the dry season.'[13]

Four years later, in 1988, another report showed that the only cattle on the land were feral – 100 unbranded beasts and none with brands. The only white occupants were two sleeper-cutter gangs and the contract musterers in the dry season. With helicopter cattle mustering now the norm, even the musterers rarely touched the ground. Some seed had been sown and some internal fencing, dams and mustering yards constructed, but the mustering yards were no longer useable and the main yards and dip had not been built. The airstrip and machinery shed were still there and, using their own money, the timber cutters had built a toilet and shower block. The report said they intended to build a house for themselves on the holding.[14] Given the state of the run it was unlikely the leaseholder would care.

The pastoralist's failure to build all the structures and maintain them gave the government, under the *Land Act*, justification to resume the land. Justice Mary Gaudron said no evidence had been presented about whether the Minister had exempted the leaseholders from fulfilling the conditions of the lease, but 'it seems that, at the very least, a decision has been made not to enforce it'.

Legal theory

In short, then, one of the parcels of land in question in the Wik case had never legally been farmed or used to pasture any animal. The only activity by non-Aborigines relating to it had been a bit of paper shuffling in Brisbane 80 years ago. The holder of the other lease had so comprehensively neglected his holding that his stock had run wild and a group of wandering timber cutters was eyeing it off for the purposes of building a hut.

In the meantime, the Wik and Thayorre people continued to live in their ancestral country, to hunt, fish, practise their ceremonies and visit their sacred sites. On the Holroyd lease they might have encountered the occasional beast or seen a helicopter fly overhead during the muster, but as their representatives argued to the High Court, nothing at all of relevance had happened to the land as far as they were concerned.

It is important to understand these facts, because they were very influential in the final decision taken by the High Court. But, as Justice Kirby pointed out with some force in his judgement, the governments of Queensland and the Commonwealth had tried to ignore these facts in their arguments:

> [To them i]t was the resolution of a conflict of legal titles which was to be decided on legal principles determining legal rights: not factual evidence regarding land use. I have nevertheless described the evidence as to the use of the land in the pastoral leases in this case because the emerging facts illustrate vividly the kind of practical

physical conditions for which pastoral leases were created by the Queensland Parliament. Those facts also demonstrate the very limited occupation of the land which was expected and regarded as normal under pastoral leases. They show how Aboriginal law and tradition could readily survive in such an environment because of the very limited contact which was inherent in these pastoral leases between Aboriginals and those connected with the lessee. The understanding of these facts helps to provide the context against which the application of legal theory must be tested in this case.[15]

Mining leases

There was another part of the claims of the Wik and Thayorre which we have not yet mentioned – their claim against two bauxite mining leases on the land. The Queensland Government had issued these leases to mining companies Comalco and Aluminium Pechiney Holdings, the former in 1957 for 84 years, and the latter in 1975 for 42 years.[16]

Part of the Wik claim, which encompassed significant portions of Comalco's lucrative mining operations at Weipa, was that the Queensland Government had not been entitled to issue those leases. The claim said that the government had flouted rules of procedural fairness and was in breach of its duty of trust to its Aboriginal constituents. The Wik were claiming title and some interest in that land or, at the least, compensation for its loss.

Comalco has already built and mined extensively on parts of their lease but has only explored other parts. The land held by Pechiney has also been explored but not yet mined. The Wik claim sought native title over the parts of the leases not yet alienated by the development of mining infrastructure.

In the judgements in the Wik case, this part of the argument became secondary to the main issue of whether or not native title had survived on pastoral leases. The judges unanimously accepted that the Queensland Government had been entitled to issue the mining leases, had done so in accordance with the law, and that the mines could be built.

The road to the High Court
Considering the basic facts in the main element of the claim, the Wik and Thayorre peoples believed they had a very strong argument that their native title had survived the issue of the various pastoral leases. But in the year after the Mabo decision and before the Keating Government enacted the *Native Title Act* in late 1993, there was only one way to pursue such an argument – they had to make a common law claim before the Federal Court.

In June 1993 the Wik peoples commenced proceedings in the Federal Court against the Queensland Government, the Commonwealth and others, including Comalco and Pechiney, claiming native title and possessory title rights over the land and adjoining sea. If their title was found to have been extinguished by the issue of the various leases on that land, they claimed compensation for damages.

The Thayorre, the Aboriginal and Torres Strait Islander Commission, some Aboriginal land councils, various other parties, including pastoralists, and almost every state and territory government realised the significance of the case and joined the argument.

When the *Native Title Act* came into force in January 1994, the Wik people made another claim under the provisions of the new Act. The judge in the Federal Court who was hearing the case, Justice Drummond, decided to hear simultaneously the arguments for both the common law claim and the claim under the Act. In the process of making his judgement he raised five central questions. As explained in the next section, the basic question concerned whether the issuing of a pastoral lease had given the pastoralist exclusive possession of the land. If the answer to that question was 'yes,' under the High Court's explanation of extinguishment, the land had been used in a way that was inconsistent with native title, and native title had been extinguished.

In January 1996, Justice Drummond did answer 'yes' to that question. He also answered all his other questions in a way that was adverse to the claims of the Wik and Thayorre. He said, citing the preamble to the *Native Title Act* and the judgements in *Mabo*, that pastoral leases conferred exclusive possession on the pastoralist, leaving no room for native title.

Both the Wik and the Thayorre people then appealed against that decision to a full bench of the Federal Court. Those appeals were removed to the High Court under that court's power to hear such matters directly.

On 12 and 13 June 1996, the various sides came to Canberra to put their cases, and on 23 December the Court produced its decision, which, by the slimmest majority of four judges to three, found, in favour of the claimants, that native title could have survived.

Depending on your perspective this decision either complemented *Mabo* and finally achieved a measure of justice for Aborigines by guaranteeing their rights of access to the vast rangelands of Australia where many still lived; or, combined with *Mabo*, disastrously upset the whole system of land law on which the Australian pastoral industry, and many other industries, are constructed.

What did the High Court actually decide?

Refining the law

Australia's governments have the right to sell and deal in this country's land because, when the first settlers planted the flag at Sydney Cove and claimed it for England, they brought with them the English common law, which enabled them to claim title over the whole land. The Mabo decision was revolutionary because the court found that this title – radical title – did not by itself extinguish native title. It was not so inconsistent with Aboriginal habitation that it would snuff out their existing right to the land and their laws, the Court said.

The question for the judges in the Wik case was to refine their understanding of which actions would extinguish native title. What exactly constituted an action inconsistent with the existence of that title? As Justice Michael Kirby put it in his judgement, the Mabo case had been a revolution – now it was time to sort out the consequences by 'reasoning by analogy from established legal authority illuminated by relevant legal history and informed by applicable considerations of legal principle and legal policy'.[17]

Nobody disputed that the direct sale of land to a person in freehold title (a fee-simple transaction) did the job of extinguishment, but nobody yet knew, because no court had specifically looked at the issue, if pastoral leases did the same thing. And even if a lease did extinguish title, what particular action taken during the course of the transaction had broken that Aboriginal link with the land? Was it the act of the Government signing the paper which conferred the lease on a pastoralist? Was it the act of the leaseholder physically moving on to the land? Was it when that pastoralist built something on that land? Was there, perhaps, extinguishment only on the actual sites of structures? If no extinguishment took place at all, what would happen to those pastoral lease-holders who had paid their rent and followed the rules? Or could native title be suppressed for the duration of a lease and revive when it ended? These were the questions the judges had to answer in Wik.

Justice Drummond's legal questions distilled these issues. The most important question was this: 'Does the pastoral lease confer rights to exclusive possession on the grantee [the pastoralist]?' The follow-up question was: 'Did the grant of the pastoral lease necessarily extinguish all incidents of Aboriginal title or possessory title of the Wik Peoples in respect of the land demised under the pastoral lease?'[18]

Justice Drummond was asking whether or not those people who had taken up pastoral leases had such firm ownership of the land that they could exclude all others, including the indigenous inhabitants, from any claim to ownership or title. It was already clear that neither governments or pastoralists had *physically* excluded the Wik or Thayorre from inhabiting the land, but it was not clear whether they had any legal right to be there, or whether they were just allowed to stay because nobody had yet evicted them.

In his answers to these questions, Justice Drummond found the leases did confer a right to exclusive possession, and therefore that the granting of them had extinguished native title.

What both he and subsequently the High Court did was to decide these issues as questions of law not of fact. This meant they had wide ramifications for all other leases in Australia which contained the same terms and conditions. However, this still left open the determination of the actual facts of the Wik and Thayorre cases. Neither court decided whether these two groups fulfilled enough of the other conditions required under the *Native Title Act* to successfully claim native title. This question is still undecided, and at the time of writing the groups were in mediation under the processes laid down by the *Native Title Act*. In order to have access to those processes, they had to agree not to pursue their claims through the Federal Court, so all parties are awaiting the outcome of the mediation.

'You've got to put up with it these days'

Will Roberts, pastoralist, 'Victoria Downs', Charleville, Queensland

' ... Mum's great-grandfather bought the property, it was run by her grandfather. In 1906 it was purchased and the stud was started in 1911. Sheep and cattle.

'There's two native title claims over it at this stage ... It's one of those things that certainly nobody wants to have hanging over their heads. I totally disagree with the whole thing but that's the way the system works and you've got to put up with it these days. I mean, you don't live in the perfect world and you've got to take a lot of these things in your stride ... I try not to worry about things that I can't do anything about, if possible. We're just leaving it up to the experts and we've got to wait and see what transpires ...

'Once the 10-point plan's put into place everybody will know a little bit more about it, but before then basically we can't go anywhere or do anything – It's beyond our control … And we've basically had no contact at all with any [Aborigines]. According to what we can get our hands on from where they were years and years ago, this country wasn't in their track, because there's basically no permanent waterholes close by here … As everybody keeps saying, a lot of these claims they are just claiming stuff willy nilly and whatever they can get they'll have.

'One of the things as far as I'm concerned that stinks about the whole system is how they've got this wonderful affinity with the land, but if somebody comes up and offers money to them they'll just sell it. I mean that's just bullshit, that's just absolutely ridiculous … One of the great problems with the Aboriginal community it's a bit like the problems we've got – there are a few people at the top who are going to cream a hell of a lot of dough out of this and the rest of them are going to be left exactly the same bloody way as they are now. It just stinks, it really does. And they're not going to be any better off, the Australian people are going to be worse off because the taxpayer's going to have to fund a hell of a lot of bloody money for nothing. I mean, this is just too ridiculous for words the way the whole bloody world's going at the moment.

'[I blame] all the do-gooders. I don't think there's any doubt about that. Nothing much has come out of all this political correctness as far as improving things. It's basically only made things worse for everybody …

'I mean, as everybody keeps saying, when Captain Cook first came here the Aboriginals lived the same as white people do now – most of them around the edge of Australia and a few on the inland. And yet we're the ones that are sort of carrying the can, so to speak, to appease the Aboriginal community. And that sort of wears a bit thin on everybody. If people in the city had the same burden to bear, so to speak, I'm sure they'd bloody squeal a little bit about it.

'We fight about what politicians are doing and can do bloody nothing about it, this is just a little bit worse than that. It's the same old story. A few pay for a hell of a lot. It's not a new situation, and you can't blame any of the city folk because they're not the ones making the rules. No, we don't blame anybody.

'I just think they ought to wake up to themselves. A little bit of common sense would go a bloody hell of a long way in a lot of these things and I mean it's just so hard to get anybody to have any common sense these days. Most of them are boffins.'

Mabo as a basis

In making his decision, Justice Drummond partly used the Mabo judgement as a basis for answers to the questions he had set. While the question of pastoral or other leases had not been fully dealt with in that judgement, some of the judges had made passing references to leasehold interests.

Justice Brennan (by 1996 the Chief Justice) wrote in 1992 that if a lease was granted, 'the lessee acquires possession and the Crown acquires the reversion expectant on the expiry of the term'.[19] That is, at the end of the term of the lease, the Crown inherited the title – an action which was considered likely to extinguish native title. Justices William Deane and Mary Gaudron said in their joint Mabo judgement that the title Aborigines might enjoy under common law would have been extinguished by 'an unqualified grant of an inconsistent estate in the land ... such as a grant in fee [freehold] or a lease conferring the right to exclusive possession'.[20]

On the basis of these two references in the Mabo judgements, two federal governments (one Labor, one Liberal) and the Federal Court all seemed confident that a lease, like freehold, would extinguish native title. Even Aboriginal leaders, while never accepting that this *should* be the case, were pessimistic that they would achieve any other outcome. By the time the High Court came to look in detail at the issue for the first time in the Wik case, both sides of politics and most of the lobby groups interested in the issue believed it would probably uphold Justice Drummond's answers to his questions, and rule against the Aborigines.

But the High Court has a history of bucking expectations. Since *Mabo*, the Court's composition had changed. The Chief Justice in 1992, Sir Anthony Mason, had retired, to be replaced by Bill Gummow. Sir William Deane had been appointed Governor-General by Keating and replaced on the Court by Michael Kirby. None of those counting the numbers to see which way the Court would jump in the Wik decision could be quite sure of the attitudes of the new judges.

In the end, Brennan, who had ruled in *Mabo* that native title had survived the Crown's assumption of radical title, ruled in *Wik* that it could not have survived the issue of a pastoral lease. He was joined by Justices Daryl Dawson and Michael McHugh. But the two new judges, and two already on the Court, Justices John Toohey and Mary Gaudron, disagreed. So, by a bare majority of four, the Court was swayed by the arguments of the Wik and Thayorre, and ruled that native title could survive.

The Aborigines' arguments
Lawyers for the Wik and Thayorre peoples made two basic arguments against the answers that Justice Drummond had given. The first was that the government had never intended that the pastoral lessees have a right to exclusive possession of the land. They argued (quoting a phrase of Justice Brennan's in the Mabo decision) that the sheer size of the leases in question meant that it would have been 'truly barbarian' if they had been intended to exclude the traditional inhabitants and turn them into trespassers.[21] If the legislature *had* intended this, it would have been written explicitly into the land Acts which conferred the leases. No such provision was there.

Their second argument was that all the conditions and reservations that various Queensland governments had written into the leases indicated that they had never intended to allow exclusive possession. If assorted timber cutters, guano gatherers, mining prospectors, government officials and musterers were allowed, if authorised, to conduct their various businesses on the lease, quite apart from the Aborigines who everybody acknowledged still lived there, the pastoralists' possession could not have been exclusive.[22]

Combined, these two arguments effectively put the position that the indigenous inhabitants had a legal right to coexist on the land. They were entitled to live, hunt and conduct their ceremonies under the law as established in the Mabo decision, not just by the sufferance of the government or the current holder of the lease.

The Wik and Thayorre also had a variety of fall-back positions. Even if the lease conferred exclusive possession, they argued, it was not the government's action of granting the lease that carried the power to extinguish their title, but any subsequent action by the leaseholder which was inconsistent with their native title rights. In the case of the Mitchellton and Holroyd River leases, the pastoralists had done so little on the land that native title must have survived. If it had been extinguished at all this could have occurred only where the buildings or airstrip had been constructed, and the rest of the land still belonged to native claimants.

Their final position was that if the Court found that the government's actual act of granting a pastoral lease was inconsistent with native title, then native title was merely suspended for the duration of the lease, not extinguished. When the lease ended or lapsed, the native title rights would revive. They argued that the Crown had a responsibility, a 'fiduciary duty', to native title holders to return that land. This duty had created the presumption that the legislature could not and did not intend to extinguish native title.[23]

The minority judgement

The Chief Justice, Gerard Brennan, was not convinced. He had written the lead judgement in *Mabo* which recognised the existence of native title, but to acknowledge these new arguments for native title surviving the issue of pastoral leases, he said, would be taking it too far. In *Wik* he agreed largely with Justice Drummond's judgement. Of the three judges in the minority, he was the only one to offer reasons

– Justices Dawson and McHugh simply agreed with his. Thus his is the only minority judgement available for scrutiny.

Brennan thought it was unnecessary for the legislature to write into its lease arrangements an explicit intention to exclude the indigenous inhabitants from their land. His argument was based on the distinction between the two types of laws which regulate the English (and therefore Australian) legal systems.

Common law is a kind of default law, born out of English custom and modified or reinterpreted over time by the reasoning of judges in various cases, which is why it is sometimes called 'judge-made' law. Overlaid on that is statute law, or law made by parliaments responding to the particular needs or wishes of the people who elect them. While statute law overrides the common law, and while judges are bound by statutes, statutory law is open to interpretation and judgement just the same as common law. And it can be interpreted in light of the general principles of the common law.

For example judges use the ordinary common law definitions of legal phrases to interpret statutes. Another interpretative tool is the parliamentary debates which occur as governments pass laws. These are supposed to give hints to the original intention of the parliament.

Justice Kirby made the point that the Wik case was very difficult because the Court was being asked to work out the intentions of parliaments in nineteenth and early twentieth century Queensland who had never conceived of native title, to see if their actions had extinguished that title: 'In this case the present must revisit the past to produce a result, wholly unexpected at the time, which will not cause undue collision and strife in the future.'[24]

The argument in *Wik* centred around whether the statutes creating the leases on the Mitchellton and Holroyd River holdings, and hundreds of others in Queensland, had conferred an exclusive right to ownership on the leaseholder. Chief Justice Brennan argued that they had, because, as a general principle, the courts should interpret statutes by reference to the same definitions as understood in the common law. In this case the word 'lease', as used in the various land Acts in question, should be understood by its common law definition, and that definition (taken from a 1909 land tenure case) is that a lease is a 'contract for the exclusive occupation of land for a determinate period, however short ...'[25]

Brennan argued that, 'On the issue of a pastoral lease under the 1910 Act, the lessee acquired an estate. There is no legal principle which would defer the vesting of, or qualify that estate in order to allow the continuance of a right to enjoy native title.'[26]

This question of the definition of the word lease, and how it might differ in common law and statute law was also a crucial element in the judgements of the four who thought native title had not been extinguished.

Brennan also rejected the Wik and Thayorre arguments that because the land was open to anybody whom the government of the day vested with the authority to traverse it, the lease was never exclusive. He said the fact that Queensland governments bothered making explicit reservations simply implied that in all other respects the leaseholder *was* entitled to exclusive possession: 'The reservation, far from implying that the lease did not confer a right to exclusive possession, implies that, without the reservation, the lessee would have been entitled to refuse entry to any person ... the restriction on use of the land was consistent with a lessee's right to exclusive possession.'[27]

As for the argument that nobody had ever properly taken up the lease, so there was nothing done on the land which was inconsistent with native title, Brennan said this did not come into it. The fact that the leases had not been taken up, or any of the other facts applying to any of the other hundreds of pastoral leases around the country, were irrelevant because 'The question of extinguishment of native title by a grant of inconsistent rights is – and must be – resolved as a matter of law, not of fact.'[28]

Brennan (and all the other judges) said that if it was left up to the facts in each individual case to decide the merits of a native title claim, the process of deciding such things would have dragged on through the courts for years. It would have been an abrogation of the duty of the High Court.

As a matter of law, then, Brennan argued that the action which had extinguished native title was not the act of the pastoralist and his herd walking on to the land and using it, it was the government's act of signing that piece of land over to the leaseholder: 'In my opinion, the lessees under each pastoral lease had possession and a right to exclusive possession at the latest from the moment when the lease was issued,' he said.[29]

Because such a lease, by the common law definition of the word, conferred exclusive title, there was inconsistency between the right of the leaseholder and the right of 'any other person to enter or to remain on the land'. If access is crucial to the exercise of native title rights, the inconsistency arises 'precisely because the rights of the lessee and the rights of the holders of native title cannot be fully exercised at the same time'.[30]

Therefore, he said, native title was extinguished.

Answering the Wik and Thayorre's fall-back argument that a lease, once it lapsed or was forfeited, would go back to native title, Brennan said 'reversion' of the title would always go to the Crown. The Crown's exercise of power over the land by issuing the lease had increased its stake in the land. So instead of the land reverting to 'radical title', which the Mabo judgement found failed to extinguish native title, the Crown, on the reversion of the lease, got back full title or, in legalese, a *plenum dominium*. That title, of course, was inconsistent with native title, and therefore also extinguished it.[31]

'It is only by treating the Crown, on exercise of the power of alienation of an estate, as having the full legal reversionary interest, that the fundamental doctrines of tenure and estates can operate,' Brennan wrote. 'On those doctrines the land law of this country is largely constructed. It is too late now to develop a new theory of land law that would throw the whole structure … into confusion.'[32]

Brennan seems to be alluding to his Mabo judgement, in which he warned against fracturing the skeleton of principle which supported the whole body of the law. A new theory of land title – that native title was only temporarily suspended, or that native title and pastoral title could coexist – would create insoluble difficulties: 'The law can attribute priority to one right over another but it cannot recognise the coexistence in different hands of two rights that cannot both be exercised at the same time ... The law would be incapable of settling a dispute between the holders of the inconsistent rights prior to their exercise, to the prejudice of that peaceful resolution of disputes.'[33]

No doubt John Howard would agree.

But even though Brennan's judgement was adverse to the Wik and Thayorre, he cannot be said to lack sympathy with the Aboriginal view. He wrote that the very principles of the law he was upholding 'may thus be thought to reveal a significant moral shortcoming'. Regrettably, however, Aboriginal dispossession was an unchangeable fact of history, and the issuing of leases was just another example of it.[34]

He also argued that, just because title was extinguished, it did not mean Aborigines would have to leave the land. Neither the Wik nor the Thayorre had ever been required to leave despite the issuing of leases. They just had no legal title over the land. As long as the pastoralist on those holdings continued to consent to the indigenous inhabitants being there, they could stay, and a leaseholder 'who took no steps during the term of the lease to exclude known Aboriginal inhabitants from the leased land, must be taken to have consented to their presence on the land'.[35]

The majority judgement
This was not enough for four of the Chief Justice's fellow judges.

'That a concept of feudal tenure brought to Australia but subjected to change through a complex system of rights and obligations adapted to the physical, social and economic conditions of the new colony, in particular the disposition of large areas of land (often unsurveyed) for a limited term for a limited purpose, should determine the fate of the indigenous people is a conclusion not lightly to be reached,' wrote Justice John Toohey in the lead judgement of the majority.[36]

He and Justices Gaudron, Gummow and Kirby found, contrary to what Brennan had argued, that a pastoral lease might restrict the rights of the native title holders, but native title could still survive and coexist; that the common law definition of a lease could not be applied unquestioningly in this case; that the Crown did not win back full title when a lease lapsed; and therefore that the Federal Court's Justice Drummond had been wrong when he had ruled that native title could no longer exist on the Mitchellton and Holroyd River leases.

Toohey arrived at his position after looking in some detail at the history of Australian land tenure, and the reasons why legislatures had invented pastoral leases instead of giving pastoralists freehold rights to the massive tracts of land in Australia's interior. He drew the conclusion that Australia's system of land law had grown up to fit conditions so unique to Australia that the feudal system of the English common law as it related to land was not adequate.

Leases, he found, reflected 'the desire of pastoralists for some form of security of title' but also 'the clear intention of the Crown that the pastoralists should not acquire the freehold of large areas of land, the future use of which could not be readily seen'. They were, he thought, a form of security for governments who might need the land at a future date for a purpose as yet unknown.[37]

Because the system of land tenure in Australia was so different from that in England, and the rules governing it so different from the English common law, it made sense to interpret differently the definitions of some common-law terms. Just as the size and uses of the leases themselves would have been unimaginable in an English context, so the words that created them also had to be taken out of their understood English common-law context.

The word 'lease', by that argument, could not be defined as conferring a right to exclusive possession. These unique leases had been created by unique statutes, and therefore conferred nothing more than 'a bundle of statutory rights': 'Pastoral leases lie in the grant of the Crown. They are the creature of statute and the rights and obligations that accompany them derive from statute,' Toohey said.[38]

As a result, each of the rights the statute gave to the pastoralist under the Queensland Acts in question had to be defined separately in each piece of legislation in order to carry any power. This was particularly the case if the words were to carry such massive weight as to dispossess whole groups of people of their traditional land. This argument reflected the position put by Justice Brennan in the 1992 Mabo judgement that, 'the exercise of a power to extinguish native title must reveal a clear and plain intention to do so, whether the action be taken by the Legislature or by the Executive.'[39]

In the light of this, Toohey said Brennan's argument in *Wik*, that merely by exercising its power to issue a lease the Crown had extinguished native title, was too simplistic: 'Where is the necessary implication of a clear and plain intention?' he asked.[40] Justice Kirby said that, given the strength of the Aborigines' link to the land, it would have taken a 'very clear law' to sever it.[41]

A search of the 1910 and 1962 Queensland *Land Acts* for evidence that the parliaments intended to extinguish title was fruitless. These Acts made no mention of the Aboriginal inhabitants, and certainly gave no indication of a desire to remove them from the land. Neither the wording of the leases themselves nor the legislation which created them indicated to the majority judges that those who had passed the laws allowing pastoralists to take up leases had ever intended that those leases be exclusive to the pastoralist.

As Toohey put it, 'There is nothing in the statute which authorised the lease, or in the lease itself, which conferred on the grantee rights to exclusive possession, in particular possession exclusive of all rights and interests of the indigenous inhabitants.'[42]

He and the other majority judges gained further evidence of this from a number of other sources. They quoted at some length the reports of the Northern Protector of Aboriginals in the early years of the century, Walter Roth, who, as explained in Chapter 1, argued forcefully for the rights of Aborigines to stay on their land regardless of whether a pastoral lease or licence had been granted over it.

They also looked to the original statute that had turned

squatters into licence holders, the *Crown Lands unauthorized Occupation Act*. This Act contained a provision that allowed the government to cancel a licence issued under it if the licensee was convicted 'of any injury committed upon or against any aboriginal native or other persons'.[43]

In an 1839 despatch to the Secretary of State in Britain, Lord Glenelg, NSW Governor Sir George Gipps wrote that the *Crown Lands unauthorized Occupation Act* had been designed partly 'for the purpose of putting a stop to the atrocities which have been committed both on [the natives] and by them'.[44]

The then British Secretary of State, Earl Grey, said in 1848 that pastoral leases were 'not intended to deprive the Natives of their former right to hunt over these Districts, or to wander over them in search of subsistence, in the manner to which they have been heretofore accustomed, from the spontaneous produce of the soil except over land actually cultivated [or] fenced in for that purpose.'[45]

As Justice Toohey argued in his judgement, 'The whole tenor of these provisions indicates a contemplation that Aborigines would be upon licensed lands.'[46]

The so-called 'reservations' in favour of indigenous people were not explicitly present in the later land Acts, but the judges argued that governments, by that stage, tacitly accepted their presence.

Besides which, the many other reservations explicitly written into the leases militated against the notion that pastoral leases were intended to be exclusive, the majority judges said. The fact that the leases explicitly allowed the land to be used for pastoral purposes only; the fact that the Crown reserved the right to permit anybody to enter the land for any purpose; the explicit orders that timber cutters, mining prospectors, guano gatherers and others be allowed onto the land; and the fact that in some cases the Crown still reserved the power to order the pastoralist to complete certain modifications to the holding, all indicated to the majority judges that the pastoralist could not truly be said to have full possession of the land. These special circumstances meant that the common-law definition of the word 'lease' could not be used.

The majority judges also found that, even if the pastoralists had exercised their leasehold interests to the fullest extent possible this would only involve the use of the land for grazing purposes. Such activity was of such limited intensity that the local Aborigines could easily continue to use the land as they always had.

Justice Kirby wrote that 'In pastoral leases of the kind described in the evidence in this case, talk of "exclusive possession" or "exclusive occupation" has an unreal quality. It may be what the law imputes to the lease at common law. But it would require very clear law to drive me to such an apparently unrealistic conclusion. The common law tends to abhor unreality, even when it is presented as legal doctrine.'[47]

The majority judges also found unconvincing Brennan's argument that merely by exercising their power to dispose of the land, the Queensland governments had extinguished native title. Toohey wrote that there was 'something curious in the notion' that native title could 'somehow suddenly cease to exist, not by reason of a legislative declaration to that effect but because of some limited dealing by the Crown with Crown land'.[48] A legislative action showing a clear intention to extinguish title was required.

As for the question about whether a lease would return to the Crown as a *plenum dominium* (full ownership) when it lapsed, or just return to radical title, the majority judges again disagreed with Justice Brennan. According to Toohey, to rule that a lease reverted to the full beneficial ownership of the Crown would 'apply the concept of reversion to an unintended end'. For the land to revert so fully it would require a clear intention, and again he found there was no evidence in the legislation of anything of the sort. It did not undermine the Crown's sovereignty for the court to rule that a lease would revert to radical title, without extinguishing native title, he said.[49]

The only concession the majority judges gave to the governments, pastoralists, miners and all the others banking on extinguishment, was that any action taken by the pastoralist on the Holroyd River lease which was inconsistent with native title would extinguish that title. So the few improvements the leaseholders had made (the airstrip, the small area sown with seed and the internal fencing, dams and mustering yards) meant that in those specific areas the local Aborigines had lost their right to enjoy native title. The act of conferring the Comalco and Pechiney mining leases on that land had also extinguished title. But in all other respects native title could have survived.

This one small caveat on the existence of native title in no way lessened the massive significance of the Wik decision to Australia's system of land law. The judges made it clear at various points in their judgements that they knew what they were doing, and were aware of the controversy it would draw down on them and the legislative pickle it would create for the government. But they went ahead anyway because, according to the four in the majority, that is the law of the land and it was their duty to state it.

'We still practise our traditional ties'

Mary-Lou Buck, Dunghutti elder, Crescent Head, New South Wales

'The Kempsey local Aboriginal land council had put in two land claims under the [NSW] *Land Rights Act*. They were not approved ... but the *Native Title Act* opened up another gateway for us. What had happened was that development had taken place on this particular area, where we had the land claims. [It was] sub-development, for housing, an extension of the township [of Crescent Head].

'When we had the land claim in, the Kempsey shire council had a meeting with the representatives of the land council and asked could they lift one of the land claims to assist them with the development of this particular township, and in particular, to establish a reservoir. And for that we would receive at least 10 blocks of land. And that did not take place. We relinquished the land claim, they built the reservoir, but we didn't receive any blocks of land or whatever. So we've disputed all that.

'So then the Minister for Conservation and Land Management put in a non-claimant application over the area, which meant that we could respond if we wanted to. We sat down and had many meetings and we decided then, yes, we would put in a native title claim. I was the one who put my signature on that claim, being from the Dunghutti Land Council. And that made the Minister's claim invalid. So we had to then turn around and prove again, once again, our traditional ties and our cultural heritage ties to this particular land. And it took us many many months to get all the documentation.

'We've lived on that land for many many years. Our grandfathers, our fore-grandfathers have lived there. We still practise our traditional ties. We still practise gathering our bush tucker. The only thing we weren't allowed to do was go onto private property where somebody's land was taken away from us, because of the legalities, we could be sued for trespass now. But it didn't stop us from practising our traditional ties in that particular area ...

'We were successful in winning that claim. People were elated. It was something new because nobody knew whether native title was going to work and we just stuck by each other all the way through ... we researched every documentation we could possibly get our hands on, the family trees, the genealogies, and produced all that as evidence.

'There's two sections of that [result]. With Section A we were compensated $736,000 because of all the infrastructure that has taken place there. And Section B, which was the undeveloped area, our traditional ties have been recognised over the whole area. And because that's not developed, any further development they would have to pay us compensation. We're not using that land for anything at the moment, because in the meantime it's up to the state government because of the compulsory acquisition that the state government had done they've taken that back. So whether they sell it off or whether the real estate people, or the Kempsey Shire Council wants to develop it in any way whatsoever they have to pay us compensation, the Dunghutti people.

'I think it can work. We can coexist. It was also part of a reconciliation process. We could have been really really nasty, said 'No, we want the thing, we don't want you to develop this town.' But because our ancestors own that land, we want to share it with everybody else, you know? And with the non-Aboriginal people we had many many many mediation meetings and it was a part of it, you know. It can coexist, alongside one another.

'I am very confident about the future. I have never given up any hope at all about the native title situation and in particular the Wik situation.'

Unanswered questions

However, the High Court did leave some of the legal implications of its decision unclear. The most obvious of these was the status of the Wik and Thayorre claims themselves.

The Court's majority ruled that the coexistence of native title and leasehold title were possible on the leases in question, but did not rule whether or not native title had *actually* survived. None of the judges took the facts as they were presented and decided that the Wik had a right to enjoy native title on the land of the Holroyd River lease, and the Thayorre on the Mitchellton lease. None of them arbitrated the dispute between the two Aboriginal parties for the section they had both claimed around the Edward River. Those decisions were left up to the Federal Court, to which the High Court handed the case again. The difference was that it had now directed the lower court as to the law.

At the time of writing, those claims were being arbitrated and details of their progress were confidential.

Justice Kirby also conceded that the Wik judgement had not answered all the questions that governments, pastoralists and the public might want to ask. Different colonial governments in different jurisdictions had dealt with the spread of pastoral activities in different ways. There were hundreds of different statutes and forms of leases still in use around the country. Each had its own system of conditions and reservations, each allowed a number of activities on the land and prohibited some others. Some statutes might have conferred bundles of rights which were much more exclusive than those in other statutes, making it much harder for native title to survive.

As a result the position of all these countless other leasehold interests could not be decided by extrapolating from the Wik judgement. According to Justice Kirby they 'must remain to be elucidated in later cases'.[50]

In effect, while the Court made a judgement based on the law applying to one particular set of Queensland leases, it left the whys and wherefores of native title on other forms of leasehold land to case-by-case legal battles in lower courts or tribunals. It would be a painfully slow process for most parties.

The judgement also left much else unanswered, or only partly answered. What exactly could pastoralists do or not do? Were they restricted to the exact activities written into their leases, or were they allowed to conduct the expanded activities they had adopted in more recent times? Exactly what rights of access and use did native title holders have? Must indigenous people be able to prove a direct and continuing physical link with the land to claim native title rights? Or was a historical link, recently severed, enough? Could Aborigines buy and sell their right over a pastoralist's land to, for example, a mining company? Did the possible presence of native title on a lease affect the value of that lease?

Justice Kirby acknowledged that the Wik decision 'introduces an element of uncertainty into land title in Australia other than fee-simple [freehold]'. This might cause some 'strife' in the future but, he said, it was necessary strife, and 'no more than the result of the working out of the rules adopted in Mabo'.[51]

Toohey's solution

Justice Toohey made the most conscious attempt among the judges to explain how the parties might approach these issues from now on, and he did it in a brief set of comments in a section entitled 'Postscript' at the end of his judgement. He conceded in this section that, despite the hope that the

High Court would 'resolve all important issues between the parties', the way Justice Drummond's questions had been framed had meant that was not possible.[52]

He took pains to emphasise, however, that just because he and his three fellow judges had found that pastoral leases did not confer exclusive rights on the leaseholder, this in no way destroyed their title to the land. All it meant was that their rights were limited to the terms of the laws that framed their leases. That is, in this particular case, they had few rights over the land other than to graze their cattle and build appropriate infrastructure to help them with that task.

He was talking about coexistence. Native title holders were entitled to enjoy their rights under their form of title, and pastoralists were entitled to enjoy theirs under the legislation. They would have to learn how to live together.

This sounded simple but, for the reasons already mentioned, it would not necessarily prove to be so. Justice Brennan had warned against the coexistence argument for just these reasons, saying it might 'prejudice ... peaceful resolution of disputes' because the law had difficulty trying to 'recognise the coexistence in different hands of two rights that cannot both be exercised at the same time'.[53]

Justice Toohey had a brief answer to this. While saying that the rights of Aborigines and pastoralists were not necessarily inconsistent with each other, he acknowledged that disputes might crop up, and his crucial formula for solving them came in this statement: 'If inconsistency is held to exist between the rights and interests conferred by native title and the rights conferred under the statutory grants, those rights and interests must yield, to that extent, to the rights of the grantees [the leaseholders].'[54]

That is, if the rights of the parties came into conflict on any point, the rights of the pastoralist would always prevail.

The Aboriginal negotiators say this is a simple dictum. It is also one they are happy to live with. After all, until now their right to be on the land began and ended with the leaseholder's whim to tolerate their presence or not.

The president of the National Native Title Tribunal, Justice Robert French, said in a press release just days after the Wik verdict was announced that pastoralists and

Aborigines on each parcel of land would have to sit down and come to agreements with each other about what they were each entitled to do on that land. Only by making agreements could certainty be achieved for both parties.

So what is all the fuss about?

Attractive land

The Mabo judgement had the general effect in 1992 of telling Australia's governments and their people that native title existed and had always done so under common law. However, its effect was limited to unalienated Crown land – land that had remained undeveloped by white settlers – because that was the nature of the Murray Islands land forming the basis of the claim. As a result *Mabo* only had a direct effect on other areas of unalienated Crown land.

There is relatively little land of this type in mainland Australia and it is land which is, almost by definition, not very attractive for development.

Four years later in *Wik* the Court said that even though white settlers had used leasehold plots in far north Queensland, native title could still exist on them. This decision potentially had a direct effect on vastly larger areas of land than those covered by Mabo – 42 per cent of the continent, and in some states 70 to 80 per cent of the land. These tracts of country have been used and are still being used. They are, therefore, of great interest and value to others – among them pastoralists, whose livelihoods depend on them, miners, because much mining activity is conducted on pastoral leaseholdings, and governments, because public works such as pipelines traverse thousands of kilometres of remote leasehold land.

The decision is of vital concern to governments for political reasons too – because many members of state and federal parliaments have country constituencies.

The combined effect of the Mabo decision, the *Native Title Act* and the Wik decision was to open a huge proportion of the continent to native title claim. The government claims it is 78 per cent, but Aboriginal negotiators say this would be the case only if every conceivable type of lease were counted. Regardless of the exact figure, one result is that the Aboriginal right to negotiate with potential developers and governments (under the provisions of the *Native Title Act*) now covers a huge proportion of the Australian land mass.

Some might argue that this is only fair, and a better deal than the indigenous inhabitants were given when the land was first alienated. But considering the fact that since the Mabo decision the government in Canberra had changed, and given the money and influence of pastoralists and other rural constituents, it was a politically explosive outcome.

Certainty

Governments and industries hate what Justice Kirby called strife, and what they call uncertainty. The way they saw it, every one of the hundreds of leasehold and licence interests granted since settlement, carried with it the danger of another legal battle. So the new Prime Minister, John Howard, just as Paul Keating had done in 1992, announced that his Government would legislate to set out the rights and powers of the various parties.

Under the circumstances created by *Wik*, legislation setting the rules of engagement is not in itself a bad thing. Without it the cases deciding these matters could drag through the courts for years. The important issue is how those rules are formulated and how certainty is achieved. If it is a question of using the new common law as the basis of an honest attempt to regulate coexistence, that would constitute justice, according to the High Court's definition. If on the other hand the legislation rides over the rights of one party because the interests and political affiliations of the other are seen as more important, then justice has not been well served.

In the weeks and months of uncertainty and rhetoric following the High Court's decision, various doom merchants predicted (just as they did after *Mabo*) that legions of farmers would be forced off their family land. Others have dusted off the hoary old propaganda about suburban backyards and water supplies being threatened.

These things cannot happen as a result of the High Court's ruling, particularly considering Justice Toohey's explanatory postscript.

On the other hand, it now seems that the Government's proposed laws make it entirely possible that Aborigines could be dispossessed of their common law rights in a way that has not happened since the early days of white settlement.

How has this come about?

3

Political Games

What is the Government's position and why?

John Howard's pendulum

John Howard's concise analysis of the Wik decision is that the High Court swung the pendulum too far in favour of Aborigines. His stated intention is to swing it back the opposite way.

This is his Government's prerogative. Australia's system of government and the separation of powers doctrine mean that statute law overrides common law. As long as the statute is in keeping with the Constitution, the Commonwealth Government can legislate away rights the High Court has discovered. But whether such an action either constitutes good and lasting law, or serves a broader notion of justice, are entirely different questions.

The Coalition Government was faced with a number of choices when the Wik decision was handed down. It could ignore the decision and allow the common law in conjunction with the *Native Title Act* (and the amendments to it already tabled) to deal with the unexpected situation. It could introduce new amendments to the *Native Title Act* to put the Wik decision into effect. Or it could pass a very short amendment that would have as its sole provision and purpose the removing of title from Aboriginal hands if a pastoral lease were involved. Such a clause might have been titled 'The Extinguishment of Native Title on Pastoral Leases'.

This last alternative was the outcome wanted by the National Farmers' Federation, the conservative state leaders and Howard's Coalition partner, the National Party. They ran a tireless campaign from very early in the piece, trying to bully the Prime Minister into bowing to their demand and swinging the pendulum as far as it would go in favour of the pastoralists.

But, as Howard was to point out much later, such a 'one-line' extinguishment of native title would change the *Racial Discrimination Act* – something he had promised during the election campaign he would not do. It would open Australia to international censure for acting so drastically against its own indigenous people, would cause domestic divisions between black and white and would result in a potentially massive compensation bill which taxpayers might be reluctant to foot. Such a provision also stood next to no chance of being passed by the Senate.

Howard and his parliamentary secretary, Nick Minchin, knew these things from the start – they had said as much in May 1996 when formulating their earlier amendments to the *Native Title Act* (described in Chapter 1). But despite this prior piece of clear thinking by the Government, it was the war of words about legislative extinguishment, driven by the cacophony from conservatives both inside and outside the Coalition, which shaped the Wik debate for months after the decision was handed down.

Howard, knowing the political risks he ran by alienating his own side, allowed the argument to continue, and at times actively encouraged it, while knowing he could not give in to the demands for extinguishment. Meanwhile he was busy casting around for a compromise that would allow him to swing the pendulum back towards the pastoralists without earning him the eternal damnation of the Aborigines, the taxpayer and the international community.

First reactions
Howard himself declined to comment on the day the High

Court dropped its bombshell, 23 December 1996. He left the comments up to his Attorney-General, Daryl Williams, who wisely said the decision was 'complex' and needed 'careful consideration'.[1]

Others were not so restrained. The premiers of Queensland and Western Australia took the earliest opportunity to demand immediate action, Queensland's Rob Borbidge calling for a summit within the month and a referendum on the issue. The pastoralists' peak national body, the National Farmers' Federation, unilaterally announced the end of Aboriginal reconciliation.[2]

The following day, Christmas Eve, the Prime Minister issued a press release describing the High Court's decision as 'disappointing'. Considering the confidence with which his legal advisers had assured him the decision would go the other way, and considering the storm that was about to erupt around him, it was a masterful understatement.

The judgement, he said, 'appears to have overturned one of the fundamental principles on which the community's understanding of native title had proceeded' and he conceded that his election policy had been 'influenced in part' by that understanding. The decision had raised 'ambiguities and questions which must be addressed and resolved'. To that end he called for talks with all stakeholders on the issue.[3]

Throughout January the calls for extinguishment from the state leaders, notably Western Australian premier Richard Court, Queensland's Rob Borbidge and the Northern Territory's Shane Stone, became ever louder and more hysterical. Howard went for his annual beach holiday at Hawk's Nest in northern NSW and in his absence, his Government remained cautious. The Acting Prime Minister, Tim Fischer, while flagging a change in the law to guarantee 'absolute certainty' to pastoralists,[4] would not talk directly about legislation to extinguish native title. His attitude was misunderstood by sections of the media, who interpreted his comments as being a signal that the Government would legislate to extinguish. Fischer made no attempt to correct that impression.

But he did take out his frustration by shooting the messenger that had delivered the bad news – the High Court.

The Government could not in 48 hours 'produce a legal magic wand to fix the uncertainty which the High Court has created progressively over a period of 48 months', he said. On 10 January he again berated the Court, saying that rather than applying the law it had indulged itself by making the law, and that parts of the judgement were 'awful'.[5] Howard backed him up on this point, saying in February that the Court had become too activist.[6]

It was later revealed that Chief Justice Brennan had responded in a letter to Fischer to the first of these attacks, saying they had damaged the Court and asking him to consider whether this was 'conducive to good government, even if an attack can gain some temporary political advantage'.[7]

Howard and Fischer were not the only two with the High Court in their sights. In keeping with former Queensland premier Sir Joh Bjelke-Petersen's attitude to the separation of powers, the current incumbent, Rob Borbidge, launched several forays against the Court. In February he called it an embarrassment, and he even came up with a plan: fixed 10-year terms for judges, a state government veto over court appointments, a new judicial watchdog and referendums to decide whether controversial judges should be sacked.[8]

Howard scotched this attack immediately and the suggestions were never seriously discussed.

Meanwhile the hard business of negotiating was beginning. A meeting of state and Commonwealth officials on 10 January was told that more than 70 per cent of Australian land – everything but freehold – was now open to claim.[9] The most conservative states (and predictably those most affected by the ruling) began to form an organised bloc. Queensland, the Northern Territory and Western Australia had a number of meetings and, by the end of January, were well on the way to forming a united view with which to put pressure on Howard.

The states' attitude

The chief activist in this united conservative position was Queensland's Rob Borbidge. By this time he had realised he was facing problems in his own state which went beyond judicial activism.

Based on bad legal advice and the preamble to the *Native Title Act*, his Government had issued 800 leases on pastoral land since 1994, mainly for mining and mineral exploration, without having given Aboriginal groups any notification of the decisions. Any potential native title holders had thus been denied the opportunity to lodge claims. If any of those mining leases extinguished an Aboriginal group's native title, the Aborigines would be able to claim compensation, and it was likely that the state would have to foot the bill.

If Borbidge had taken the simple precaution of notifying the potential native title holders, under the provisions of the *Native Title Act*, or even of seeking indemnity from compensation from the mining companies, he would have had nothing to worry about. But his Government had been so frightened of admitting even the vaguest possibility that title might exist on pastoral leases that it had taken neither of those precautions.

Borbidge was understandably desperate for the Commonwealth to solve his problem by retrospectively removing the rights he had already damaged. His tactic was to embark on a ruthless campaign of pressuring Howard to bend to his will.

Borbidge's Minister for Natural Resources, Howard Hobbs, started the ball rolling in early February by announcing the halting of any substantial development of pastoral leases. He also froze the issuing of new leases and the renewal of most existing mining leases. It turned out later that this order was issued without legal advice,[10] and it cost miners and pastoralists dearly. It was reversed in March.

Throughout the debate Borbidge was the most vocal in his opposition to the Commonwealth's plans, the most critical of Howard and Fischer, and the most adamant that extinguishment was the only option. He was the last, and the most grudging, to accept Howard's plan when it appeared that the Prime Minister would not back away from it.

The other conservative states needed little convincing to adopt Borbidge's line. From their first meetings their common position was that the Commonwealth must legislate to extinguish native title. The states, in return, would legislate (if such legislation did not already exist) to allow Aboriginal people access rights to some leasehold land.[11] This scheme might have mirrored other statutory access arrangements in some other states, but it would not have allowed Aborigines any form of title, ownership or autonomy over land.

On 5 February the conservative states released a joint discussion paper with their version of a solution. They wanted the Commonwealth to put a 1 January 2000 deadline on all native title claims, to pass a law extinguishing native title on pastoral leases and replacing it with limited statutory access rights, to reduce Aboriginal rights to negotiate, and to limit compensation payments.[12]

Their 'solution' would, by 2000, have snuffed out every right to native title which the Mabo and Wik judgements had established, for the payment of limited compensation. It would have outraged the Aboriginal community and the international community, and probably breached Australia's international human rights obligations. It was the response which the cooler heads in the Coalition had already rejected (though they were keeping silent about that fact) and the one which Aborigines feared most. In short, it was tailor-made to inflame the debate.

The National Party

But the states were not the only parties intent on whipping things up. One of the biggest hurdles to the speedy resolution Howard was so keen to reach was his own Coalition partner, the National Party.

On 7 February Don McDonald, the party's president (and among Australia's largest leaseholders; see Appendix 2), entered the fray, issuing a statement calling for the Government to extinguish native title and pay compensation. He even advocated raising taxes if necessary to cope with the payments.

The Nationals' leader, Tim Fischer, caught between a rock and a hard place, talked more obliquely, saying that 'the body of evidence, the weight of opinion, is pointing to clear-cut legislation. There are no soft options.'[13] Despite his hayseed image (he ran the country via mobile phone from the top of Mount Kosciusko while Howard was holidaying in January), Fischer is an adept political operator. His trick throughout the debate was to talk in code. The 'no soft options' line was designed to hint to his country constituents that he was batting for legislative extinguishment, while leaving enough room for him to support Howard's inevitable position which was to fall just short of it. It was a fine line which Fischer, under enormous pressure, trod for almost six months.

The pressure from his own party was constant: the president of the Queensland Nationals, David Russell, called for a conversion of leasehold land to freehold, because leasehold was an anachronism, and no longer suited to 'modern pastoral husbandry and land management'.[14] At a 1 March National Party federal executive meeting Fischer faced the first of many rumblings against his leadership;[15] the party warned of a national crisis unless the Government legislatively extinguished title, with the federal president, Don McDonald, saying the whole nation was 'on the brink of closing down'.[16] On 18 March Queensland Senator Bill O'Chee threatened to resign from the Nationals if Howard's plan codified Aboriginal and pastoralists' rights and did not extinguish them, and in mid-April Fischer got a luke-warm reception at the Queensland party's conference with only 3 out of 200 people standing to applaud him.[17]

In mid-May Fischer, sick of the constant rumblings from his party room, challenged his detractors to move against him if they dared. None spoke up and his leadership was safe.

The National Farmers' Federation

But the National Party was not the only conservative organisation to pile pressure on the Coalition. The National Farmers' Federation conducted a vicious campaign in country areas to convince the average farmer that extinguishment was the only reasonable outcome.

The farmers' peak national body had moved a long way from the compromise position it held in 1993. Its then leader, Rick Farley, had left the organisation soon after the *Native Title Act* was passed. He is now a member of the

Council for Aboriginal Reconciliation. The new leadership team (which consistently made snide public references about having been sold out by Farley after Mabo) was much more uncompromising. It demanded nothing less than exclusive occupancy for pastoralists.

On 20 March its campaign reached its nadir with the launch of a television advertising campaign on all major networks to back its claims. These ads, in black and white, portrayed the Australian land tenure system as a grim version of the 1970s party game, Twister. The combatants were a black child and a white child, and the black was clearly getting the upper hand. (A later news release explained that, under the rules of Twister, because both kids fell over at the end of the game, it meant both had lost.)

The NFF also wrote an open 'Dear John' letter to Prime Minister Howard (presumably implying the romance was over) demanding forceful action on Wik. The full-page letter was published in every major newspaper.

While the NFF president, Donald McGauchie, said the campaign was aimed chiefly at city dwellers, it was complemented by an intensive scare campaign run in country areas. McGauchie told audiences across the country that the Wik judgement had made pastoralists into second-class citizens and removed 'one of the most fundamental tenets of ... society – the freedom to manage'. The NFF claimed the High Court's decision drastically reduced the value of pastoral land, even though the Australian Institute of Valuers and Land Economists said repeatedly that native title posed no threat to land management or planning on pastoral leases.

Speaking in Brisbane in May, McGauchie made one of his more extreme statements, implying that native title claims would cut off water, power, gas and other services to Australia's city dwellers. He even resurrected an old bogey from the 1993 campaign, saying that the 'residents of Sydney and Melbourne have no reason for optimism' that the title over their own homes and backyards were safe.

Perhaps worst of all, the NFF consistently conflated the interests of farmers with those of leasehold graziers. It is true that in the flurry of native title claims all over Australia since

1994 many non-freehold farms have been claimed, and some have many more than one claim over their land. These claims, as they are required to be under the *Native Title Act*, are for exclusive possession, which can be frightening for farmers.

But the reality is that none of those claims will be successful. The High Court has shown great reluctance to interfere with the rights of white Australians, and has agreed that Aboriginal title exists only around the edges of other existing forms of title, and only if the Court thinks there is statutory space at those edges. Native title is almost certain to be defined in terms of strong existing physical links to land. In the densely farmed southern states, therefore, there is very little room for native title – it is bound to be extinguished.

It could be argued that the NFF's duty was to explain to its rural constituents the reality of the Wik decision. There is much to explain, and much ignorance and understandable fear to overcome. Instead, it set about a deliberate course of frightening these constituents with a campaign of misinformation and exaggeration. The NFF, the National Party and other alarmist players, like the Graziers' Association, seemed to do little but reinforce each other's hysteria.

According to the NFF's former leader, Rick Farley, its campaign's most obvious effect was to talk down the value of its constituents' properties.[18]

The Minerals Council of Australia

Among all this shouting, one traditionally conservative group deserves quite an honourable mention – the miners.

In the 1993 native title negotiations mining lobbyists had been among the strongest critics of *Mabo*. Hugh Morgan of Western Mining Corporation had demanded that a referendum be held on native title, and John Ralph at CRA had tried to frighten the Government by saying the Mabo decision had created uncertainty which threatened billions of dollars of mining investment.[19] The central lobby group, then called the Australian Mining Industry Council, had run a lengthy fear campaign insisting that native title prevented development and did no good to anybody.[20] In short, they had played a spoiling role. As a result the then Prime Minister, Paul Keating, left them almost entirely out of the talks and they ended up with limited opportunities to have their view incorporated in the legislation.

Since then the miners, represented by a renamed peak body, the Minerals Council of Australia, have realised their folly and come to the table. They attended the stakeholders' meetings sponsored by the Council for Aboriginal Reconciliation and had begun negotiating the fine details of how native title agreements could provide certainty for both sides.

CRA (now teamed with British mining company RTZ) had also seen the light. Its negotiations to win approval for its $1.1 billion-dollar Century Zinc mine in Cape York had been long and tortuous. It had endured inflammatory comments by Aboriginal negotiators, broken agreements and ham-fisted attempts by governments (both the Commonwealth and Queensland) to force the issue, and still had enough faith in the *Native Title Act*'s procedures to complete negotiations.

When the Wik decision was announced, this faith was reflected in the public position the miners took.

On 22 January, at the Wik summit in Cairns, the executive director of the Council, Dick Wells, acknowledged that the conversation between Aborigines and miners since 1993 had led to greater good will on both sides and the development of mutual respect. At the beginning of his speech he did something the NFF still has not done: he acknowledged the High Court's decision that native title was a coexisting common law right. He recognised the strong prior link of Aborigines to their land and aspired to 'a good long-term relationship between industry and indigenous communities'. He put strongly the view that, in pursuit of that relationship, discussion and cooperation were needed even more than in the past.

His argument was essentially practical, and in the firm interests of the mining industry. Australian mining companies were competing in an increasingly aggressive global market, and they needed certainty of title. A lawyers' picnic about extinguishment or effective extinguishment of common law rights was not the way to achieve that certainty. The miners, with the enthusiasm of converts, had taken up the cause of negotiation.

At his first meeting with Howard on 4 February, Wells said much the same thing: the industry wanted certainty but not extinguishment. The states' plan was a short-term fix which would 'fall over in the courts', he said. What he did want was for Howard to agree to validate the mining leases that state governments had granted since 1994 on pastoral land.[21]

In April, against the tenor of the 10-point plan, Wells explicitly supported the Aborigines' right to negotiate on pastoral leases. This was the provision in the *Native Title Act* to which the miners had been most vehemently opposed only three years earlier. Again his rationale was essentially practical: Aborigines denied the right to negotiate would launch court challenges against mines on pastoral land, and the Senate would obstruct any move to curtail the right to negotiate. Any of these things could make it difficult for mining companies to come to agreements with other stakeholders and be allowed to go about their work.[22] It would create uncertainty rather than prevent it.

Many are still suspicious of the miners: some Aborigines believe they are saying one thing in public, but pushing their old conservative agenda in private. Some believe they want an end to the right to negotiate because that would take out one major step in the complex process of setting up a mine. But the mining industry's public rhetoric, at least, does not support these theories.

Judging by the statements made in public, the politics of native title seem to have done a strange switch: the farmers are now the arch conservatives and the miners the moderates.

Tough political times in Queensland

As the Aboriginal negotiators kept saying, the High Court had guaranteed that the rights of pastoralists would prevail over those of the Aborigines. If that was the case, why was the reaction of the National Farmers' Federation so hysterical? Why was the ruckus from the National Party and all the other conservative elements, particularly in Queensland, so loud?

The answer has two main strands. There were a number of factual problems but, more importantly, a variety of political problems.

The main factual problem was that the High Court had ill-defined the rights of both sides. Some modern pastoral enterprises were conducting many more activities on their land than they were strictly authorised to do by the bundle of statutory rights conferred by the original leases. Legal advice told the pastoralists and their representatives that it was uncertain whether they could legally sink bores, begin agricultural enterprises, clear and burn, or make their homestead into a bed and breakfast. Some moves to diversify pastoral enterprises, which governments had been actively encouraging to insure against bad seasons, were suddenly put in some legal doubt.

But those things could have been negotiated. Aboriginal negotiators were happy to allow the pastoralists to diversify to a reasonable extent as long as the pastoralists were happy to allow them the enjoyment of their native title. These possibilities were on the table as part of the debate as it began to move into its more sophisticated stages. They were being discussed in the stakeholders' meetings convened by the Council for Aboriginal Reconciliation, before the NFF's advertising campaign precipitated the withdrawal of the Aboriginal negotiators.

The real reasons the issue prompted such apparent fear among pastoralists and members of the National Party were political, and the political problems were worst in Queensland. There were several elements involved.

Tim Fischer and the National Party had given almost unwavering support to Howard's gun law reforms in the wake of the Port Arthur massacre in April 1996. Fischer had stood firm against a loud and hysterical opposition movement in his electoral heartland (who could forget the little-Hitler jibes against Howard, or the bullet-proof vest he wore at one rally?).

That issue had won Fischer some respect in the cities but enduring enmity in the country and parts of his own party, because many saw him as having sold out to Howard and the city-based Liberals. So when the Wik decision was released, and Fischer was equivocal about whether to support extin-guishment, the conservatives in Queensland thought they could see a pattern: Fischer sells out again. It was enough to earn him earfuls of abuse and hints of various leadership challenges. All those putting pressure on him were telling him to lend legitimacy to the calls for extinguishment.

The second factor in the politics of this issue involved Rob Borbidge's extraordinarily tenuous grip on government in Queensland. Borbidge's National Party governs by the grace of one independent member, Liz Cunningham, in that state's one-house parliament. Speculation was rife in Queensland early in the year that Borbidge was looking for a trigger for an early election to increase his majority. If he could scare enough Queenslanders into thinking a vote against the National Party was a vote against extinguish-ment, he could be confident that an extra few seats would be his.

The third factor was Pauline Hanson. While her direct effect on the Wik debate has been minimal, her indirect effect has been huge. Her meetings in 1996 had attracted large numbers of enthusiastic National Party members around the country. This was particularly so in Queensland. But when she launched her party, One Nation, in April, she suddenly became an even bigger threat. The National Party's Queensland director, Ken Crooke, said at the time that Hanson's party could, by taking votes from the Nation-als, cost the Queensland Government its uncertain grip on power.[23]

In effect the Nationals and Hanson were playing to the same audience, but she seemed to be doing it more effec-tively by complaining directly and strongly about migrants and Aborigines. The National Party was simply borrowing some of her tactics in its approach to the Wik debate, in the attempt to win back those who had crossed to her side.

This situation found its most persistent expression through Federal National Party Senator Bill O'Chee, one of the squeakiest wheels on the subject of Wik. O'Chee faces re-election at the next Federal poll and, as the last of the Queensland Nationals elected, he would be the first to go if the Hanson effect eroded his party's power base. His extreme response to Wik and his threats to resign from the Coalition if it refused to extinguish native title were, at least in part, an attempt to win back his own voters from the Hansonites by being 'more conservative than thou'.

For months on end early in 1997, all these political stoushes raged around rural Australia. It was the biggest in-fight among the parties and lobby groups of the right that Australia has seen since the failed Joh-for-Canberra push cost John Howard the 1987 election.

The heat generated successfully put the Government, Howard and Fischer particularly, under intense pressure to extinguish native title.

Howard's diplomacy

When Howard returned from holidays on 20 January 1997, and took back the reins from Tim Fischer, he walked into the early rounds of this fight. He immediately called a meeting of the state premiers and chief ministers for 22 January.

Emerging from that first meeting, his words indicated that, like Tim Fischer, he would seek to find his way through Wik's challenges by talking in code. While promising nothing concrete he offered solace to those demanding extinguishment by refusing to rule out any option, and, crucially, by not denying that he planned to amend the *Racial Discrimination Act*. 'If you're asking me for a guarantee that we won't touch existing legislation, I can't give that,' he told reporters outside the meeting.[24]

From the start, Howard, like Keating after the Mabo decision, took direct responsibility (and the political risk) for the negotiations, rather than delegating it to his minister, John Herron, or his parliamentary secretary, Nick Minchin. Howard was keen to make a start, saying as soon as he arrived back in Canberra that he wanted the issue resolved quickly. On 9 February he set a deadline of four weeks.[25] He set up a unit in his department, the Wik Taskforce, to advise specifically on the issue and to help him in negotiations. He pursued a punishing schedule of meetings with all the stakeholders. Some meetings lasted up to five hours as the parties argued complex issues.

But a rapid solution proved elusive. On 10 March, his first

self-imposed deadline, Howard conceded that Wik was the hardest problem his government was facing.[26] He imposed another deadline, Easter, just three weeks later at the end of March. As it happened, his final position, the so-called 10-point plan, was not arrived at until the end of April.

However, an early draft of the plan made its debut during a meeting with the state and territory leaders at the Lodge in late March. His position achieved no agreement – the premiers were still hoping for extinguishment. Howard agreed at that meeting to consider the premiers' positions.[27] He also announced that he expected an agreed solution in two weeks.

Three days later, on 24 March, the Aboriginal negotiators, the National Indigenous Working Group led by Noel Pearson, threatened to walk away from the process after seeing some details of Howard's package. The following day the stakeholders' meetings fell apart as Aboriginal negotiators reacted to the NFF's advertising campaign and refused to have any further dealings with the organisation.

But Howard ploughed on with his plan. On 11 April it was announced as a '7-point plan'[28] and over the next weeks its important details were spelled out in various newspaper articles. On 15 April, Cabinet discussed the issue. Howard put to the meeting the 7-point plan,[29] but by the following day it had grown to 10 points. This was reported to be an attempt to win greater support from both Queensland Nationals and Aborigines.[30]

Throughout this period Howard's rhetoric was still firmly aimed at allaying the mounting fears of his own political allies, the Nationals and pastoralists: 'I am not going to sell them short, I am not going to sell them out, I'm not going to let them down,' he said.[31]

But in Queensland, Premier Borbidge was moving much faster than Howard. He tabled legislation on 1 May which would allow 3000 leaseholders to convert 22 million hectares, or 15 per cent of Queensland, to freehold, and thereby extinguish native title. The pastoralists could pay for the upgrade with interest-free loans, supplied by the Government. A cash purchase would earn them a 25 per cent discount.[32]

Proving that justice, as well as government, hangs by a thread in Queensland, Liz Cunningham, the independent who holds the balance of power, rejected the legislation. This was not because of its wholesale effect of extinguishing native title, but because it would have financially benefited too many members of the Queensland National Party Government. (It is also likely that any such Act, if passed, would have run foul of the *Racial Discrimination Act* which, as a Commonwealth Act, is beyond Borbidge's power to amend.)

Finally, by the end of April, Howard's message that he was determined to deliver a package favourable to pastoralists, began to sink in. The National Party's federal president, Don McDonald, said Howard's plan might be good enough: 'As long as the 10-point plan presents extinguishment and exclusive rights to pastoralists, then we will look at it,' he said.[33] But Rob Borbidge was still not convinced. He described the plan as 'cute' and reiterated his call for extinguishment.[34]

It was the same day Pauline Hanson's book *The Truth* was revealed to contain a claim that Aborigines had been cannibals.[35]

On 1 May, the Aboriginal working group finally found the negotiations impossible, and withdrew from them. They sent Howard a letter saying that, although they had sat through hours of meetings, he seemed more concerned to put his views to them than to negotiate terms. They told him he had shown a lack of good faith.[36]

This withdrawal had little effect on Howard, perhaps proving the Aborigines' point. He plugged on, taking his plan to the Coalition's backbench committee on Aboriginal affairs. This group, led by Western Australian MHR Wilson Tuckey, had previously strongly criticised Howard and called for extinguishment. While Howard did not win the committee's immediate agreement to his plan, it was not immediately condemned.

On 6 May, the day before the Cabinet meeting which was finally to discuss the 10-point plan, the pressure on Deputy Prime Minister Fischer reached its heaviest. He signed a National Party paper calling for its members to cross the floor and vote against the Government unless Howard agreed to extinguishment. His running orders from his two separate bosses, the Prime Minister and the National Party, seemed completely irreconcilable.

But despite the National Party's threats, on 7 May Cabinet agreed that the 10-point plan was the right answer to the problems posed by the Wik decision. Fischer explained to his party that he had been rolled in Cabinet.

As part of its decision and as a result of negotiations with the states, Cabinet also agreed to a clause to underwrite 75 per cent of the cost to the states of compensating Aborigines for the loss of their title. Some Aboriginal negotiators see this as the worst element of the whole plan because, while the states have always had the power to acquire land and thereby extinguish native title, the cost of the compensation bill has prevented them. With the Commonwealth's guarantee, that option will now be open to all the states. The states, as has been seen, are not overly sympathetic to Aboriginal rights, so they are likely to be keen to take Howard up on his offer.

What is in the 10-point plan and the legislation?
The following is an explanation of the 4 June version of the plan and the amendments to the *Native Title Act*, issued on 27 July and tabled on 4 September, which implement it.

1. Validation of acts/grants between 1 January 1994 and 23 December 1996
The first provision is intended to rescue Rob Borbidge and any other state premier who wrongly assumed they could allow mining or exploration leases on pastoral land without consulting those who might be Aboriginal owners. It retrospectively makes valid any of those leases issued between the commencement of the *Native Title Act* and the Wik decision.

The government who allowed the lease to go ahead would have to pay compensation, but under the provisions negotiated with the state premiers, the Commonwealth would underwrite that compensation, paying 75 per cent of it.

The Queensland government issued about 800 such mining leases between 1994 and late 1996.

2. Confirmation of extinguishment of native title on 'exclusive' tenures

The government proposes to put 'beyond doubt' that certain types of land tenure extinguish native title. Freehold, residential, commercial and public works are included in this. This would also apply to some agricultural leasehold land, to the extent that exclusive possession 'must have been intended' by the statute which created it.

Existing claims over those kinds of land would be able to be struck out, and schools, hospitals, roads, railways and stock routes would be put out of the reach of native title claimants.

Also excluded from native title claims will be land granted by one government to another, whether or not the use of that land would allow the coexistence of native title.

3. Provision of government services

If native title claims, or the possible existence of title, is preventing a government from providing legitimate services (like water supply, power and so on, especially in rural and remote areas), the Act would ensure that those activities could take place. This would not necessarily impede native title, but if it did, compensation would be payable.

4. Native title and pastoral leases

This is the most important of the provisions in the 10-point plan, and the most contentious.

The Government intends to extinguish native title if it is inconsistent with the rights of the pastoralist – for example, if a pastoralist has improved the land, or erected buildings. This seems to be in line with the High Court's decision in Wik. But while the High Court did not rule on whether or not native title would revive after such a building fell down, or the land was abandoned, the

Howard plan provides for native title to be extinguished forever on those areas. Aborigines argue it should just be suppressed.

Point 4 also defines what activities a pastoralist can undertake on his or her land. It does so according to the definition in the *Income Tax Assessment Act 1936*. This allows a pastoralist to: cultivate land; maintain animals or poultry for the purpose of selling them; conduct fishing operations, forest operations and horticulture; and manufacture dairy produce. The Government then added another permitted use: farm-stay tourism. It is a much broader definition of land use than the High Court found in any of the Queensland pastoral leases it examined, and broader than the 'bundle of statutory rights' which constituted most leases in other states. In effect this provision increases the pastoralist's rights over the land in most jurisdictions. A pastoralist conducting any of those activities, whether or not the lease explicitly allowed it, would not have to ask the permission of the local Aborigines, and the conduct of those activities would extinguish native title.

The two most dangerous elements of this plan are contained in point 4. The first is that it broadens the opportunities for state governments to upgrade title to perpetual or 'exclusive' leases, or freehold. The *Native Title Act* already allows a state government to compulsorily acquire land for public purposes (roads, dams, pipelines and so on), but this expands it massively, allowing land to be acquired for any purpose – even just because a pastoralist wants to upgrade his or her leaseholding to freehold. The Federal Government has agreed to pay 75 per cent of the states' compensation bill to native title holders for any such upgrade. The pastoralist upgrading the lease would be required to pay a fee – a 'betterment' charge. But that charge is to be set by the state government, and any such government wanting title extinguished over large areas of land could simply offer terms or conditions so favourable to the pastoralist that he or she could not turn it down.

The Commonwealth Government argues that this will

not happen.[37] Firstly, they say, pastoralists on the whole
cannot afford to pay betterment and secondly, the
Commonwealth intends to put some kind of lower limit
on the fee a state government can demand. If a state
charged an outrageously low betterment fee, the
Commonwealth would not pay its 75 per cent of the
compensation. The Commonwealth also argues that the
states, ultimately, do not want to lose control of the land
completely by converting it to freehold ownership.
However, whatever sophisticated arguments the Government employs, there is no doubt that any such upgrade
would breach the *Racial Discrimination Act* by allowing
the rights of Aborigines to be interfered with where those
rights exist only because of their race. The Commonwealth is not bound by that Act because it can override it
with legislation at any time, but it has promised in an
election not to interfere with it, and it could be argued it
is bound by fairness and international law not to change
it.

The other most dangerous item in this plan is the
Government's intention to abolish the right to negotiate
on pastoral leases. Howard fears that, because a much
greater proportion of the country is now open to claims for
title, the right to negotiate provisions of the Act will
become unwieldy, time consuming and a detriment to
business, particularly the mining industry.[38] So if a
government or a pastoralist wants to allow mining on a
certain piece of land, Aborigines will have no right to
negotiate terms, even if they have proven native title
rights. If they oppose the mine, their opportunity to argue
their case is no better than the leaseholder's. All they will
have access to are 'alternative procedural rights'. These
differ between states, but are generally confined to
appeals to bodies like the Administrative Appeals
Tribunal, and to compensation.

The Attorney-General, Daryl Williams, said in his
second reading speech when tabling the amendments on
4 September that Aborigines on pastoral leases had fewer
native title rights to enjoy than Aborigines living on
vacant Crown land, 'at best, only coexisting rights', so

therefore should have less ability to negotiate what happened to those rights.[39] This is no more than a government reward for past dispossession. It is consistent with the Howard Government's view that the right to negotiate is a special Aboriginal right that no other group of people has. Their moves to water it down or remove it entirely are done in the name of equality and workability.

5. Statutory Access Rights

As a sop to indigenous inhabitants, registered native title claimants who meet the more stringent registration threshold test would be guaranteed access to the land they are claiming, but only if they can demonstrate that they already have physical access to it. The Aboriginal negotiators say this rewards pastoralists who kicked indigenous people off their land in the past, by allowing them to continue to deny access to the original inhabitants, even if they have a strong emotional and historical connection.

If the native title holder succeeds with a claim, the court which determines the title must set out exactly what the Aboriginal group is allowed to do on the land. Even after this, the pastoralist's rights would still prevail over any surviving native title rights.

6. Future mining activity

The Federal Government would hand to the states its power over mining activity on pastoral land. Under the plan the states would be able to deal with mining applications using their own legislation 'provided they give native title claimants and holders the same procedural rights as other parties with an interest in the land'. Compensation, 75 per cent guaranteed by the Commonwealth, would be payable if native title was later found to have existed.

7. Future government and commercial development

This section broadly relates to the right of governments to buy land on behalf of private individuals for commercial projects. If this happened on vacant land in a town or city (for example, on town commons, some of which have been subject to native title claims in more heavily populated areas), native title claimants would have no right to negotiate. If it happened outside the town, the claimants would still have the right to negotiate, but only if they satisfied the tough registration test.

If the government wanted to acquire the land to provide government-type infrastructure (roads, pipes, dams), Aborigines would have no right to negotiate. Acquisitions of leasehold land could be passed to the states and, again, Aborigines would have no rights of appeal against such an acquisition other than the procedural rights enjoyed by the leaseholder.

8. Management of water resources and airspace
The Government is taking this opportunity to assert its right over fisheries and water. Some native title claims have been made over water, since for coastal Aborigines it is an integral part of their survival, and many waterways are the subject of Dreaming stories, but the Government will pre-empt such claims by putting beyond doubt the ability of Governments to regulate and manage water.

According to the plan, 'This certainty can be achieved without extinguishing native title (and incurring a potentially substantial compensation liability)'. This is because no court ruling has found that native title exists on waterways, and Point 8 effectively cuts off any such future finding. (Native rights over water and fishing have been acknowledged in Canada, the US and New Zealand.)

The plan will likewise make any future claim for airspace impossible.

9. Management of claims
The Government will introduce a sunset clause over all claims under the *Native Title Act*, which allows only six years from the enactment of the amendment for claims over land to be lodged. Claims for compensation would have to be lodged no later than six years after the action which gave rise to the claim.

Aboriginal negotiators say this is an ill-advised amendment because native title is a creature of the common law. The *Native Title Act* provides the best way governments have yet found of dealing with claims, and all a sunset clause will do is force all claims back into the courts.

The processes of the National Native Title Tribunal would also be shortened, for the sake of speed, and the states encouraged to manage claims within their own court and land management systems.

10. Agreements
The Government also proposes to introduce measures to help the process of negotiating voluntary but binding agreements as an alternative to more formal native title machinery, and agreements would be strengthened to provide certainty against future legal claims challenging them. This provision was included after lobbying by the Aboriginal negotiators.

The 10-point plan also makes it clear that the Government will make legal aid funding more readily accessible for pastoralists responding to claims. Farmers have rightly complained in the past that they have been unlikely to receive legal aid funding to defend their rights, whereas most Aboriginal claimants have had access to some form of funding or legal assistance. The Government's amendments would prevent courts awarding costs against either party.

Is the Government's position fair?
The amendments which the Government issued on 27 July for discussion and tabled on 4 September basically implement the 10-point plan, but, as one Aboriginal negotiator said, 'Where they've had the chance to be bastards, they have been.'[40]

For example, while native title claimants will, as the Government promised in the 10-point plan, have access rights to their land, this will only occur if they have 'regularly had physical access' to it up until 23 December 1996, the day the Wik decision was handed down. An ATSIC critique of the legislation said this formulation was 'unduly restrictive', and that statutory access rights should be available to all native title holders who pass the registration test.[41] Aborigines claiming native title will have only three months to prove their physical connection to the land if a miner is also interested – this could be extremely difficult to do. The six-year sunset clause is considered to be another excessive attempt to erode existing rights.

Another critic of the legislation, Professor Garth Nettheim, of the Indigenous Law Centre at the University of New South Wales, said the amendments created a 'new statutory animal' – a 'previous exclusive possession act'. This provision will allow the states and territories to say that certain activities have extinguished native title forever. On land ranging from freeholdings, commercial leases and residential leases, to land used for community purposes and public works (like memorials), native title will be extinguished beyond any hope of revival. Any land next to public works that was used in that construction would likewise extinguish it. State and federal governments would also have the power to write a list of interests which conferred exclusive possession and thus extinguished native title. Professor Nettheim feared government bureaucrats would be able to list anything they wanted and the Federal Court would be forbidden to accept any claim over such land.

'Without abolishing native title permanently', Professor Nettheim said recently, the Government's amendments would 'marginalise it to the extent that it doesn't get in the way'.

Nevertheless the 10-point plan is not as extreme as the position Howard was being pushed to adopt.

Under Howard's plan Aborigines would still have a right to claim native title on pastoral leases, though the process they would have to follow would be much more restrictive. While claims were being processed, and if they could prove a physical connection to the land, they would be able to use the land as usual. If they were actually found to hold title they would have some limited say in what happened on their land in the future. It is not yet clear what rights courts would actually find to be conferred by native title, but these are likely to be hunting, fishing, gathering, camping and ceremonial rights. Daryl Williams also made it clear in his second reading speech that most acts done in the future were subject to a 'non-extinguishment principle,' which meant that, while a piece of land was subject to a lease, licence or other government grant, native title was temporarily suppressed for the period of the grant, and would revive at the end.[42]

So a few would end up better off than they are today, with their title confirmed and rights to their land that they have never had before. Those rights would be limited by the activities of the pastoralist and the decisions of a court, but they would be more certain than at any other time since white settlement.

But in most other ways the Government's plan would diminish the Aboriginal rights which the High Court described as existing in common law. This is something Howard freely admits when he says he is swinging the pendulum back, away from Aboriginal rights. The most damaging aspect of the plan is that, although Howard has not explicitly legislated to extinguish native title on leasehold land, it is clear that this plan allows wholesale extinguishment to take place.

A state government – one run, perhaps, by Rob Borbidge – could encourage pastoralists on vast areas of land to upgrade their leases to freehold. While the pastoralist would have to pay a betterment fee for any such upgrade, the government could provide cheap loans and discounts to make it easier to pay it. While the compensation bill attached to such upgrading would have made it impossible to undertake before Howard's 10-point plan, the Commonwealth's offer to pay the states 75 per cent of the cost of compensating the native title holders makes the crucial difference.

Aboriginal negotiators fear that the offer of assisted upgrades to leasehold provides the mechanism under which a wholesale transfer of rights from indigenous people to private interests could take place – a transfer funded almost entirely by the taxpayer.

Indeed, for the states it might look like a relatively cheap and convenient way to rid themselves for all time of the problems they think Aboriginal land claimants create for development. (It might actually create more problems for them than it solves, by giving pastoralists vastly more rights over the land than they have ever had before. In the future the pastoralists, now with freehold rights, might be the ones blocking development and claiming compensation. But it remains to be seen if any state government is this far-sighted.)

Keating's legislation invented the 75–25 formula to help state governments pay compensation when they validated actions taken before the Mabo decision had shown those activities to be wrong. Howard's offer opens the way for assistance to be paid for actions taken in the future – when it is clear they curtail rights discovered by the High Court. While Howard's advisers believe this will not happen,[43] and while his Wik Taskforce is attempting to find ways to prevent it, it is unwise to legislate to allow the possibility of something in the hope that it will not take place.

It is this possibility, contained in point four of the 10-point plan, which has the potential to alienate vast areas of land from native title. And this is the provision which, above all others, has indigenous Australians so angry.

But Howard argues that his plan is based on principles of fairness. Explicitly allowing Aboriginal title holders access to administrative appeals mechanisms is to treat them fairly, he says, because then they have exactly the same access to rights as the leaseholder. But in suggesting that Aboriginal titleholders are exactly equal to leaseholders, he downgrades the value of native title, which the Court found was more analogous to the governments' rights to the land than the leaseholders'. This 'equality' also does not recognise the special relationship the High Court acknowledged existed between Aborigines and their land. By putting that relationship on a par with that of the pastoralists, it downgrades that, too.

Also in the name of equality, the 10-point plan would curtail the Aborigines' right to negotiate under the current Act. This right was given Aborigines in 1992 when they demanded a right to veto development on land, so it was already a watered-down version of what they wanted. But

Howard and many members of his party have always considered this to be a special right for Aborigines, and discriminatory because other landowners do not have access
to it. Under their plan it would be abolished in the name of
'fairness' and 'equality'. The fact is, however, that if even
the right to negotiate on a proposal to take away indigenous
native title rights is removed, Aborigines get very little at
all out of the *Native Title Act*, and nothing that resembles
fairness or equality.

A clue as to whether or not the plan is actually fair might
be seen by looking at the way Howard sells it to different
audiences. To some audiences, like those of talkback callers
to right-wing Sydney radio host, Alan Jones, he boasts about
how harsh he has been towards Aborigines:

> I mean, just remember that I'm the Prime Minister who
> took money out of the ATSIC budget. I'm the Prime
> Minister who was attacked by the media of this country
> for [doing so] ... I'm the bloke that's been under
> constant attack from Aboriginal leaders for being
> insensitive to their situation ... I'm also the Prime
> Minister who belonged to the party that voted against
> the *Native Title Act* in 1993 ...
>
> I want to get the record straight: any suggestion that
> we have perpetuated the Aboriginal industry is wrong.
> Any suggestion we have continued the ludicrous
> practices of Robert Tickner when he was Aboriginal
> Affairs Minister are wrong. But equally, they are
> Australians like you and me. And when you are dealing
> with matters that affect the Aboriginal people, like
> native title, they are entitled to be consulted, they are
> entitled to be treated decently and ordinarily, like
> everybody else.[44]

But to the mainstream press Howard's position has been
more conciliatory. At the press conference when he issued
the 10-point plan he called it a 'fair outcome because it
guarantees that titleholders, whether they are indigenous
titleholders or other titleholders, will be treated in a completely fair and equal fashion'.[45]

This argument, it seems, is the same in principle as that put by Pauline Hanson when she says that Aborigines are privileged because some welfare mechanisms favour them. Under this definition of fairness, everybody is entitled to the same-sized slice of the same pie. It is a radical redefinition of the notion, away from the old definition in which fairness included the attempt to redress disadvantage. Under the new definition, taken to an extreme, a profoundly disabled child would be treated in the same way as a child with normal physical ability, or a family with two unemployed parents would be given the same child endowment as a high-income family. That would be called fair and equal treatment.

What is the Aborigines' position?

'Be moderate'
Indigenous Australia was tempered by the Mabo negotiations into a strong political force in this country.

But by the end of 1996 it was a lobby which knew enough of politics to realise that there had been a change in the guard. It had got nowhere by cursing the new Coalition Government for its deep cuts to ATSIC, and had made no headway against Howard's obvious reluctance to engage in the reconciliation process. Threats to boycott the Olympics, and accusations of racism did not work – the Government was not listening and, importantly, it seemed that mainstream Australia was not listening.

It was clear to one of the chief Aboriginal negotiators, Noel Pearson, the day after the High Court handed down its Wik judgement, that to win anything from this process, the indigenous position had to be moderate. He wrote in *The Australian* that day that the Wik claim was 'modest and conciliatory'. Pastoralists, he said, should be able to 'punch their cattle, enjoy their lifestyles and livelihoods on lands they have, without doubt, grown to love and wish to keep', but Aboriginal people should also be able to enjoy their homelands according to their 'ancient relationship'.[46]

The High Court had, again, agreed with the indigenous

position, but Aborigines knew that by claiming the high moral ground and refusing to budge, they could alienate large sections of the population. The reason the Aboriginal viewpoint is relatively absent from the above analysis of the overheated politics of this issue is that theirs has been the only voice not shouting.

The National Indigenous Working Group on Native Title (formed in April the previous year to respond to Howard's earlier amendments) realised they had some hope for a negotiated settlement if they convened quick talks between the stakeholders – themselves, the farmers and the miners. The Council for Aboriginal Reconciliation had convened a successful set of meetings in 1995 and 1996 which, while they did not always end with agreement, had at least prompted useful dialogue between parties who had been in combat at times in the past. So the Cape York Land Council quickly organised a summit meeting between 20 and 22 January for the stakeholders.

Negotiations in this forum continued on and off until the end of March, when the NFF's advertisements hit the airwaves. At that point the Aborigines pulled out, saying they could no longer negotiate with a group employing such tactics.

But on the whole, they themselves stayed remarkably calm. In a draft communications plan, a Sydney advertising agency advised its Aboriginal clients to remain competent, 'concerned and caring', honourable and credible, and, above all, calm. They should stake out the 'middle ground, rather than try[ing] to position ourselves as the "best"'. The purpose was to 'positively influence the response of the Government', enhance the credibility and trust in indigenous Australians, and mobilise support for Aboriginal Australia.[47]

Consistent with this approach, the (Coalition-appointed) chairman of ATSIC, Gatjil Djerrkura, put to Howard a statement of general principles at a meeting in February. This comprised a set of minimum outcomes that Aborigines would accept. Aborigines asked that:
- the Commonwealth adopt a non-discriminatory policy in dealing with the property rights of all Australians

- there be no extinguishment or impairment of native title
- there be no implied or direct amendment to the *Racial Discrimination Act* or deviation from its principles
- the Commonwealth respect the native title decisions of the High Court
- there be no amendments to the *Native Title Act* which erode existing indigenous rights, particularly in relation to the right to negotiate and the effective extinguishment or impairment of native title rights by the expansion or conversion of pastoral interests
- there be no amendments to erode the Indigenous Land Fund, set up by Keating for Aborigines to buy back land
- the Commonwealth agree to a process for negotiations with indigenous people on native title issues.[48]

As was to be made clear, the Government would ignore many of these positions, particularly the fifth.

Instead of legislation overriding their rights, Aborigines asked that those rights be defined through negotiation between the parties. They were prepared to consider a higher threshold test for claims, which would prevent the vexatious claims, but allow all the legitimate ones. They also requested a minimum code of the rights that Aborigines and pastoralists were entitled to enjoy. This would take the form of a series of trade-offs that Aborigines and pastoralists could negotiate. The pastoralist could expand his enterprise to irrigate and crop the land, and, in return, the Aborigines' prior ownership could be recognised and sacred sites protected.[49]

But by the end of March, the Aboriginal negotiators were wondering if their message was being heard at all. On 24 March the working group threatened to walk away from the negotiations after seeing early details of Howard's package. These details included requiring Aboriginal claimants to have a physical connection test to the land (which Pearson argued rewarded pastoralists for past dispossession and governments for taking indigenous children from their mothers), and ruling out the right to negotiate on pastoral leases.

What is in the Aborigines' 6-point plan?

It was clear by this stage that the pressure on the Commonwealth from the states and the various conservative lobby groups was going to be hard to match by the force of moral persuasion. But, faced with the need to produce a clear position, the Indigenous Working Group plugged on. On 16 April, as the Cabinet was beginning to firm up the Government's position, the indigenous group publicly issued its detailed response to the Wik decision. It was called 'Coexistence – Negotiation and Certainty'.

Like the Government's, its list of proposals had grown somewhat, and also included some responses to issues which were outside the strict confines of the challenges thrown up by the Wik decision. The position was a relatively comprehensive submission which asked Prime Minister Howard to look at the whole issue of native title and how he dealt with it. It was based on certain key principles. These included: no test by which Aborigines have to prove a physical connection to their land before they can win native title; no sunset clauses on claims; no extinguishment of title without the informed consent of the title holder; and no precluding towns, cities or waterways from claims or the right to negotiate.

The following is a précis of the Aboriginal negotiating position.[50]

1. Pastoral leases and coexistence

The working group accepted the existing rights that pastoralists had over their land, including their rights to operate and develop their leases without the requirement to negotiate with native title holders about such uses. They also made clear that they accepted the position of Justice Toohey that the pastoralists' rights would prevail over those of native title holders where they were in conflict. The group said it would support legislative confirmation of 'the existing legal rights of pastoralists under their leases'.

However, they also wanted the existing rights of native title holders to be confirmed in the amended legislation.

The submission said the problem was 'basically one of legislative drafting'. The working group was concerned to ensure that the legislation confirming the rights of pastoral leaseholders not reduce the native title rights which had been discovered to exist in the common law. The working group wanted to work closely with the Government in the drafting of these codified rights.

However, the submission opposed the use of the *Income Tax Assessment Act*'s definition of primary production, which Howard's 10-point plan had used, because this was the 'widest definition possible' of a pastoralist's rights, and allowed the immediate upgrading of leases to 'de-facto freehold titles'. Apart from the native title issues involved, the Aborigines argued that this would create other public policy problems for state governments, not the least of which would be environmental problems from possible over-use of the land.

Protection of native title rights could be achieved by allowing Aborigines immediate rights of access to land once they had successfully lodged a claim to the land, and access to the right to negotiate. Indigenous people found to be in possession of native title would be able to expand their native title rights (allowing them to do more things with the land) either through agreements or by appealing to the Federal Court. Their sites of heritage value would be protected. They agreed to a more stringent threshold test for native title claimants, but opposed the very tough test set out by the Government in its existing amendments to the *Native Title Act*.

The rights of pastoralists would also be protected by the legislation. The Commonwealth Minister could outline in legislation the activities which a pastoral lease allowed the leaseholder to carry out. Anything beyond this would have to be negotiated by the pastoralist with the native title holder, and would have to have a minimal effect on native title.

The main mechanism for dealing with native title claims should be agreements between Aborigines, pastoralists and other interested parties. These agreements, which are already provided for under the

Act, could cover whole regions, or be on a lease-by-lease basis. The Act could also include some standard, or 'off-the-shelf' sets of rights, which parties could refer to when they were making their individual deals.

Importantly, the right to negotiate would be triggered when a pastoralist wanted to clear land, undertake tourism activities, remove natural resources (like timber) or change or upgrade his or her tenure, and did not have those rights already. Aborigines, in other words, would have a say in whether or not those activities took place, and under what conditions. If the native title holder and the pastoralist agreed, they could provide opportunities for diversification of the pastoral lease under the agreement they had negotiated.

The Government's plan ignored this position by proposing the complete removal of the right to negotiate over pastoral leases.

2. Amendments to the *Native Title Act*
This section of the working group's submission covered the Government's 1996 amendments. Briefly, it made some detailed comments about the threshold test for native title, proposing a test lower than that suggested by the Government, but higher than that in existence currently under the Act. It opposed most aspects of the downgrading of the right to negotiate, encouraged the use of native title agreements, and generally supported the upgrading of Aboriginal representative bodies to negotiate on behalf of native title claimants.

3. Validation of mining and other interests
This section answered point one of the 10-point plan, which proposed a blanket validation of mining leases approved on pastoral leases since the *Native Title Act* had come into being in 1994, even though Aborigines had not been given the opportunity to negotiate on those grants. The indigenous submission said any such validation was unnecessary and rewarded governments who had avoided the provisions of the *Native Title Act* since 1994.

While generally acknowledging that leases approved

since 1994 would have to be made valid, it did not agree that the miners should benefit straight away, while the negotiation of compensation for Aborigines could drag on for years through the courts. Where native title rights had been impaired by the grants of land, it proposed a speedy process be set up to determine compensation.

In the case of land granted for other purposes, like government-to-government grants, the process of negotiation should be undertaken, since there was no urgent need for the land to be available immediately.

4. Indigenous economic empowerment package
This section set out a method for money to be set aside to permit Aborigines to participate in developments and investments on their native title lands.

5. Fast tracking the recognition of native title on Aboriginal reserves and leases
Land already set aside for indigenous people, like reserves and Aboriginal-owned land, particularly in the Northern Territory, should be given a streamlined procedure to determine native title.

6. Heritage protection and native title
Since the protection of Aboriginal heritage sites is crucial to the enjoyment of native title, the working group called for a national model for protecting such sites.

The farmers' response
In response to this paper, the National Farmers' Federation put out a press release saying it 'could not find a single proposal ... which delivered to the farming community anything provided by the 1993 agreement to the *Native Title Act*.' It said the paper tried to 'fossilise the rights of the pastoral industry' by only allowing leaseholders to undertake activities 'prescribed by turn of the century laws and statutes which don't take into account today's business realities'.[51]

The Aborigines lose patience
On 18 April, two days after the public release of the working

party plan, and as the Prime Minister's own plan was beginning to take its final shape, Howard again met with the Aboriginal negotiators, this time for five hours. A representative
of the Central Land Council, Bruce 'Tracker' Tilmouth,
came out of that meeting calling Howard's plan 'virtual
extinguishment'.[52]

Finally, after all the control and moderation, the dam burst
and some stronger rhetoric was let loose. The indigenous
group warned of a massive compensation bill, international
action in the United Nations, and possible South African-
style trade sanctions. It was clear their patience had finally
run out.[53]

Deputy Prime Minister Fischer responded, telling the
Victorian National Party conference that these threats were
a 'betrayal' of Australians.[54] The continual threats by the
pastoralists had, presumably, been fully acceptable.

The rhetoric on both sides continued to toughen in the following days as more meetings failed to change Howard's
position. The Aboriginal negotiating group accused the
Prime Minister of talking endlessly to them about his plan,
but not actually negotiating and incorporating their concerns.
On 1 May the indigenous working group wrote to Howard,
saying it was 'still willing to negotiate but at this moment it
has no evidence of good faith, and no encouragement to do
so'. The group proposed to suspend further discussions 'until
it receives your detailed response' to its detailed position.[55]

Howard responded by releasing his 10-point plan.

In his column on 3 May, Alan Ramsey of the *Sydney Morning Herald* quoted notes which the negotiators had made
when Howard was speaking during one of these meetings.
The notes recorded Howard's response to a question about
whether he had read the Aborigines' detailed position.

'I read a lot of documents,' said Howard. 'I don't agree
with a lot of points in your document. We've reached a point
where all parties have to put aside rhetoric and get on with
it. We don't agree with your right to negotiate. No-one else
has that right. You didn't have that right before the *Native
Title Act* or *Wik*. The Government doesn't agree with it. Five
of the six states don't agree with it. The pastoralists don't
agree with it. They want extinguishment. The states want

extinguishment. What the Parliament will do, I'm not sure.'

It was clear by this stage that Howard wanted to take the toughest line he could without legislating to extinguish, and that nothing the Aborigines could say to him would sway him.

The Aboriginal verbal response stepped up another notch. The Social Justice Commissioner, Mick Dodson, had this to say about the pastoralists: 'I mean, these aren't your little battlers who have to bring in a few farm stays to make the pennies meet. They haven't got the seats out of their trousers as it were. It's public land, that they're renting to graze stock. It's an opportunistic land grab. Some of the richest people in this country ... are wanting a form of title over public land for a song. We must all be concerned by that.'[56] Aborigines, he said, would have no choice but to embark on a campaign of litigation if the plan was adopted.

Mick Dodson's brother, Pat, the then chairman of the Council for Aboriginal Reconciliation and the most moderate of the moderate Aboriginal leaders, also joined the attack. On 25 May he said the Government's Wik plan was equivalent to the poisoning of waterholes, and was all about extinguishing native title.[57] (This attack permanently lowered the high esteem in which he was held by the Government, a fact that was clearly demonstrated in December when he tried to put conditions on his continued leadership of the Council. Dodson said he wanted an official apology for the former policy of removing Aboriginal children from their families, and an assurance that the Government would protect indigenous rights in the Wik legislation. The Government turned him down on both counts and, when he asked for his position back, told him they had already replaced him with Evelyn Scott.)

On 15 May a group of Aboriginal landowners at a summit in the Kimberley spontaneously set fire to a copy of Howard's 10-point plan.[58] On 21 May the working group briefed a group of foreign diplomats in Canberra on the effects of the plan. Mostly the diplomats said the question of native title was the responsibility of the Australian government to sort out.

The indigenous working group then put its energy

towards convincing the majority of the Senate to amend Howard's legislation—an effort that, in the end, proved successful.

What happens next?

The Senate
On 27 June 1997, Howard publicly released his draft legislation, and embarked on a further series of negotiations. In the time between the release of the 10-point plan and the release of the draft legislation, the National Party, the Government's backbench committee and Rob Borbidge were all persuaded to make public statements which were at least reluctantly in support of Howard's response.

The plan was tabled in the House of Representatives on 4 September. The document that went to parliament included about 300 pages of detailed amendments. The Act it was amending was only 127 pages long.

It then went to the Joint Committee on Aboriginal Affairs and Native Title for examination. The committee comprises members of all parties in both houses, but Government members are in the majority. On 27 October the majority reported, offering only one very minor change to the legislation, even though many of those appearing before the committee opposed the 10-point plan. The majority of legal opinion indicated that it would probably breach the *Racial Discrimination Act*. But the Government and the committee preferred to rely on other unpublished opinion that it did not.

One submission was never presented to the committee— that of the Australian Law Reform Commission. It was suppressed by the Attorney-General's department because it disagreed with the Government line. The submission said the legislation's two objectives (to preserve native title but to hem it in with restrictions) were 'mutually inconsistent', and the means by which they were to be achieved 'inadequate and counterproductive'.[59]

However, one positive thing came out of the hearings. The Labor Party demonstrated, after much internal wrangling, that it would hold firm on native title, refusing to bow to pressure from its Queensland and Western Australian branches, or to internal polling that said land rights was an electoral loser. Labor would oppose key elements of the 10-point plan and back the position of the Indigenous Working Group. It produced one of two dissenting reports to the main committee report.

Two days later, on 29 October, the Act passed the House of Representatives, with Labor opposing it, and it was sent to the Senate. There the real battle was to take place.

Senator Brian Harradine

Independent Senator Brian Harradine is not renowned for making his opinion known early in a debate. If, as he did in this case, he alone holds the balance of power, he is inclined to keep quiet about his vote until he has heard the arguments from both sides on the floor of the chamber. But late on the night of 25 November, the first night of the Senate debate on the Wik legislation, Harradine stood to say the Government's legislation needed 'substantial amendment' before he would vote for it. Rejecting the Government's line that this was an issue of property rights, not a moral issue, he argued that Aborigines deserved some measure of justice.

It became clear the following day that Tim Fischer, the Deputy Prime Minister, and Nick Minchin, Howards native title spokesman, were not prepared to accept any such argument. While Howard was out of the country they reintroduced the old furphy that native title threatened the backyards of Australia, presumably in an attempt to lend legitimacy to their position in the wake of Harradine's attack on it.

On 30 November John Howard took to the national airwaves to tell the nation that the issue needed to be 'fixed' immediately, and that his legislation, unamended, was the way to do it. Kim Beazley followed the next evening, saying that the legislation should be changed and rendered more just. In Wik, he said, Australia faced 'the question of our history and our national honour'.

With these entreaties ringing in his ears, on 1 December Harradine voted down the first of the Government's provisions—the sunset clause that would allow only six years for land claims to be lodged under the amended *Native Title Act*. The following day he revealed the rest of his amendments, calling them the 'essential minimum for justice and fairness'. It hurt him not to attempt more, he said, but he was seeking to find a compromise that even the Government might accept.[60]

Among his most significant changes was support for the Aborigines' right to negotiate on pastoral leases. Without that, he said, native title was in effect meaningless. He also agreed to allow native title to revive when a pastoral lease expired (instead of being extinguished permanently); to prevent pastoralists extending their activities beyond those allowed in their lease without first negotiating with Aborigines; and to enable Aborigines who had been locked out of pastoral properties to make native title claims, even though they could not prove full physical connection with their land.

Over the next few days he modified some of his positions after hearing argument on the floor of the chamber. Notable among these changes was his increased support for the right to negotiate, allowing Aborigines to negotiate with miners both at the exploration stage and the exploitation stage of mining. He also supported the inclusion of a clause that made the Bill subject to the *Racial Discrimination Act*. As a later Commonwealth Act, the amended *Native Title Act* would normally have overridden the earlier *Racial Discrimination Act* wherever they were inconsistent. Labor's amendment, supported by Harradine, reversed that, making the race Act prevail whenever the working of Howard's Act was discriminatory.

On 5 December, after 56 hours of debate, the Bill passed through the Senate. Despite its losses, the Government had had many wins: all its own amendments had passed and Harradine had voted the Government's way 125 times to deny minor party amendments, compared with only 53 votes in support of them. All 15 of Harradine's own amendments were carried.[61]

The Aboriginal negotiators said it was nowhere near what they wanted. Harradine had voted to validate the thousands of exclusive possession leases issued after the Keating Government's Act had passed. He also voted to allow pastoralists to upgrade their leases to freehold without reference to native title; to cap the compensation that Aborigines could be paid for the freehold value of the land; and to deny protection of Aboriginal heritage when governments wanted to use land.

Both the shadow Attorney-General, Nick Bolkus, and Harradine said the Government had won seven of its 10 points, and pleaded with it to accept the changes in a spirit of compromise.

But Howard refused to do so. The very next day, 6 December, he called a special Saturday sitting of the House of Representatives and sent the Senate's changes there immediately. The House rejected almost all. The 10-point plan goes before the Senate for the second time in March 1998.

Under Australia's Constitution, all members of the House of Representatives face the polls at a normal election, and only half the Senators. But if a piece of Government legislation is rejected twice by the upper house, the Government can dissolve both houses and send every member of parliament to an election. If the Coalition won such an election, the Constitution would allow Howard to put the disputed legislation to a joint sitting of both houses. Under a Coalition Government, a joint sitting would almost certainly pass the 10-point plan unamended.

Some fear a double dissolution election would inflame racist sentiment in Australia and damage the country forever, both internally and in the eyes of the international community, but such an election has a number of advantages for the Government.

Firstly, despite the boost Cheryl Kernot's defection has given to Labor, Liberal opinion polling indicates that public support for Aboriginal land rights is restricted to a small number of 'politically correct' city-dwellers. Howard believes he can do very well in a poll where Wik is a major issue. Secondly, Howard thinks that sticking to his guns on this issue, and winning it, could help dispel the perception among the public and members of his own party (some of whom want his job) that he is a weak, poll-driven leader. Thirdly, if it had a renewed electoral mandate without the restrictive promises Howard made to win the 1996 election, the Government could push through a number of other controversial changes, like stronger industrial relations law or tax reform. Howard, Peter Reith and Peter Costello all began 1998 by publicly spruiking major changes they have not yet been able to achieve. Some have suggested the Coalition will campaign hard in support of the Wik legislation in the conservative regions, and in support of tax reform in the cities.

If all the minor parties and Brian Harradine hold firm to their positions in March, Howard could, and probably would, call an election any time before the end of October 1998. His rhetoric has certainly been strong: he said he was prepared to hold such an election rather than accept substantial amendments to his legislation.

The Opposition has also spoken strongly, passing a pro-Aboriginal resolution at its national conference in January. The Democrats and Greens will not back down, and given Harradine's speeches during the first Senate debate it would be extraordinary if he changed his mind when threatened with an election. The other independent Senator Mal Colston appears to be out of the picture, with Howard vowing not to accept his vote.

At this stage a double-dissolution election seems entirely possible. In that case, the most likely scenario is that the Government would win, with a reduced majority, and its 10-point plan would pass unadulterated at a joint sitting, becoming the law of the land.

'I still feel like I'm a wandering soul'

Carol Kendall, Worimi woman, Sydney

'I was separated from my family and my people at birth. And as a separated person, part of finding your identity is to establish your belonging place—that is the area you come from. For a person who has been separated from family that it is very hard, but you have to draw on strength and courage to go and do that.

'It is like coming home to yourself and your family.

'And it's really hard with the native title legislation like it is: it's exclusion again, and it's divisive, like we're standing on the outside again and looking in.

'My people are the Worimi people from Port Stephens, in NSW. And being from the east coast, through colonisation there is a lot of dislocation and fragmentation of information … I'm not a member of that land council, and I don't live in that area, but that is where my ancestors come from. And you may have people sitting on land councils whose cultural ties and blood ties don't come from that area, and it's difficult because they are deciding if you belong to the community. And if you have no community because you are just finding yourself, it is very difficult, because you could be interpreted as a johnny-come-lately.

'I was adopted by a non-Aboriginal family in 1951, right at the height of the assimilation policy. I was of fair skin. I grew up in the western suburbs of Sydney. I was placed with a loving adoptive family. There was never any open racism— there were some Victorian attitudes but no outward derogatory things said. My adoptive parents were of Christian origin, strong Christians, and Christian thinking was, 'We need to save these people' …

'There were many difficulties and internal struggles finding my natural family. When I did find them, for me it was like coming home. It was like coming home to myself. But at times I still feel like I'm a wandering soul, because I have no way of establishing continuing connection to land, which is necessary under the native title legislation …

'There has to be some way of determining connection to land for removed Aboriginal people and some way of identifying who came from this land. It is a necessary thing for removed people to establish their custodial rights. But the policy is exclusive. It stops us again because we were the ones who were removed.

'I feel really sad because we've got a policy again that is dividing us, where we would like to be recognised as a part of a whole. All policies must extend to people who were separated from their families. We can't be excluded any longer ...

'When I knew I was Aboriginal it was just an emotional rollercoaster. Elation that I could identify as being an Aboriginal person. Before that I hadn't identified with any culture or any person. I found out when I was 21 that I was Aboriginal. I was seeing an Aboriginal man, and I brought him home to meet my adoptive mother and father, and that was a dilemma for them because they didn't know if we were related.

'And then there was sadness and anger because I hadn't been able to grow up with that knowledge. I was confused in myself because of that lack of information. I went through a period of anger because I had grown up without knowing who my parents were ... I had to work through that anger.

'The healing process doesn't stop. It's a continual journey, something that I'll be on for the rest of my life.

'I found my natural mother. It was just euphoric. It was really like being reborn, I guess, like all of a sudden lights went on ... I had a mother, brothers, sisters—I found out my grandfather was Fred Maynard, one of the first Aboriginal activists in NSW in the 1920s. It was like opening a whole new world.'

A constitutional challenge

Labor thinks there is one other card it can play—a constitutional challenge to the amended Act. The shadow Attorney-General, Nick Bolkus, argues that the power the Commonwealth was awarded in 1967 to legislate on Aboriginal affairs (enshrined in section 51 of the Constitution) can be used only for the good of indigenous people. A test case (involving the Howard Government's legislation to allow the Hindmarsh Island bridge to be built) is before the High Court. If the court finds that the Commonwealth is allowed to act only for the benefit of Aborigines, Aboriginal groups will challenge the amended *Native Title Act* on the same basis.

If the Wik legislation is challenged under this law, the

Government will argue firstly that the 1967 constitutional amendment allows the Commonwealth to make any law regarding indigenous people, whether or not it benefits them, and secondly that the *Native Title Act*, as amended, will still act for the overall benefit of Aborigines.

Labor's deputy leader, Gareth Evans, believes another ground for challenge is under the international Convention for the Elimination of Racial Discrimination, made law in the *Racial Discrimination Act* through the external affairs power (s.51 (29) of the Constitution).

As he pointed out, 'If the Government's legislation goes through in its present form but is challenged in the courts, as it will be, and found invalid, as it is quite likely to be, everyone will be back to first base'.[62]

From here

Predicting the future is dangerous, and it is doubly dangerous trying to predict the future of a debate as complex and multi-faceted as this one. But it is beyond question that if we create a future in which we remain wilfully blind to the rights of indigenous Australians, we condemn ourselves to repeat the sins of the past.

Aboriginal Australians have already suffered massively at the hands of colonists, and the actions of subsequent governments have done little to reduce that suffering. Many Aborigines enjoy few of the services and utilities that other Australians take for granted. White Australia has removed their access to land and to a traditional way of living. For many it has removed their Dreaming, and failed to replace it, or even to recognise the magnitude of the dispossession.

Native title, at least for those living in remote areas, seemed to hold the promise of a new way forward, and the High Court had shown the way. A lucky few indigenous people, it seemed, could escape the fate of dispossession and hand-outs because the English law had finally recognised what they had known all along—they had a law of their own, and it entitled them to land in this country.

The Wik decision expanded that promise to a whole new realm. It allowed Aboriginal access to the vast rangelands of Australia, the pastoral holdings which are at the centre of the white myths of pioneering, mateship and triumph in adversity. It challenged the lawmakers to attempt, in good faith, to find a new way to define how two peoples could coexist on the land, it challenged pastoralists to embrace those who coexisted with them, and it challenged the public and businesses of Australia to be patient while these changes were made.

If any of those groups, for reasons of greed, selfishness or political expediency, refuse to take up those challenges, our nation is diminished.

We are in grave danger of that outcome.

The Coalition Government talks about addressing the key needs of Aboriginal people. These it identifies as physical needs: health, education and housing. While these are indisputably important, they are not the whole story. They are the needs the Government has defined on Aborigines' behalf.

Indigenous Australia itself sees other needs: justice, equity, the recognition of rights to their law and religion—and the recognition of rights to their land.

That land was taken in one invasion 200 years ago. It would be a further invasion to now remove those rights by legislation. It would show we have not come far in that time.

Notes

Chapter 1 – Matters of History

1   *The Wik Peoples v. The State of Queensland and others* and *The Thayorre People v. The State of Queensland and others*, Matter Nos. B8 and B9 of 1996, 23 December 1996, p. 175. All references are to the unpublished version of the judgement, hereafter abbreviated to *Wik* (1996)

2   *Mabo v. The State of Queensland*, 3 June 1992, pp. 31–2. All references are to the unpublished version of the judgement, hereafter abbreviated to *Mabo* (1992)

3   *Mabo* (1992), p. 27

4   *Mabo* (1992), p. 16

5   *Mabo* (1992), p. 48

6   *Wik* (1996), p. 24

7   *Wik* (1996), p. 24

8   Frank Brennan, *One Land, One Nation: Mabo – Towards 2001*, UQP, Queensland, 1995, p 70

9   *Native Title Act 1993* (Cwlth), s. 223(1)

10   Frank Brennan, *One Land, One Nation*, p. 69

11   The preamble to the *Native Title Act 1993*

12   Special conditions in a lease, issued 6 May 1931 under the Queensland *Land Act* 1910 to 1930, cited in *Mabo* (1992), p. 61

13   *Mabo* (1992), p. 62

14   *Mabo* (1992), p. 109

15   *Wik* (1996), p. 55

16   A. C. and G. W. Millard, *The Law of Real Property in NSW*, 1905, pp. 5–6, cited in *Wik* (1996), p. 135

17   *Wik* (1996), p. 57

18   *Wik* (1996), p. 50

19   Justice Gaudron in *Wik* (1996), pp. 109–10
20   Despatch No. 65, Sir George Gipps to Lord Glenelg, 6 April 1839, cited in *Wik* (1996), pp. 66–7
21   Despatch No. 134, Earl Grey to Governor Sir Charles FitzRoy, 6 August 1849, cited in *Wik* (1996), p. 67
22   Annual Report of the Northern Protector of Aboriginals for 1900, Queensland, *Votes and Proceedings* (1901), vol 4 at 1335–37, cited in *Wik* (1996), p. 187
23   Australian Law Reform Commission, *The Recognition of Aboriginal Customary Laws*, vol 12, 154 to 55, cited in Frank Brennan, *One Land, One Nation*, pp. 90–1
24   The National Indigenous Working Group, *Fact Sheet 3, The Coexistence of Native Title on Pastoral Leases*, May 1997, p.1
25   *Mabo* (1992), p. 62
26   *Mabo* (1992), p. 101
27   The preamble to the *Native Title Act 1993*
28   *Wik* (1996), p. 191
29   The Federal Coalition's Aboriginal and Torres Strait Islander Affairs policy, 1996, s. 4-1, p. 8
30   Coalition policy document, 1996, s.4-1, p. 9
31   Letter from Wilson Tuckey to John Howard, *Re: Mabo and Aboriginal Land Rights Legislation*, 7 May 1996, leaked to journalists
32   Government discussion paper, *Towards a More Workable Native Title Act: An Outline of Proposed Amendments*, May 1996
33   Nick Minchin, Press release, 8 October 1996

Chapter 2 – The Wik Decision

1   *The Wik Peoples v. The State of Queensland and others* and *The Thayorre People v. The State of Queensland and others*, Matter Nos. B8 and B9 of 1996, 23 December 1996, p. 188. All references are to the unpublished version of the judgement, hereafter abbreviated to *Wik* (1996).
2   *Wik* (1996), p. 89
3   *Wik* (1996), p. 89
4   *Wik* (1996), p. 89
5   *Wik* (1996), p. 89
6   *Wik* (1996), p. 89
7   *Wik* (1996), pp. 109–10
8   *Wik* (1996), p. 91
9   *Wik* (1996), p. 113
10   *Wik* (1996), p. 203
11   *Wik* (1996), p. 203
12   *Wik* (1996), p. 203
13   *Wik* (1996), p. 204
14   *Wik* (1996), p. 204
15   *Wik* (1996), p. 205

16   *Wik* (1996), pp. 226–35
17   *Wik* (1996), pp. 189–90
18   *Wik* (1996), p. 2
19   *Mabo v. The State of Queensland*, 3 June 1992, p. 62. All references are to the unpublished version of the judgement, hereafter abbreviated to *Mabo* (1992).
20   *Mabo* (1992), p. 101
21   *Wik* (1996), p. 8
22   *Wik* (1996), p. 9
23   *Wik* (1996), p. 8
24   *Wik* (1996), pp. 202–3
25   *Landale v. Menzies* (1909) 9 CLR 89 at 100–1 per Griffith CJ, cited in *Wik* (1996), p. 201
26   *Wik* (1996), p. 26
27   *Wik* (1996), p. 11
28   *Wik* (1996), p. 27
29   *Wik* (1996), p. 23
30   *Wik* (1996), p. 27
31   *Wik* (1996), p. 33
32   *Wik* (1996), p. 34
33   *Wik* (1996), p. 27
34   *Wik* (1996), p. 39
35   *Wik* (1996), p. 28
36   *Wik* (1996), p. 70
37   *Wik* (1996), p. 57
38   *Wik* (1996), p. 59
39   *Mabo* (1992), p. 53
40   *Wik* (1996), p. 80
41   *Wik* (1996), p. 205
42   *Wik* (1996), p. 70
43   *Wik* (1996), p. 66
44   Despatch No. 65, Sir George Gipps to Lord Glenelg, 6 April 1839, cited in *Wik* (1996), pp. 66–7
45   Despatch No. 24, Earl Grey to Governor Sir Charles FitzRoy, 11 February 1848, cited in *Wik* (1996), p. 67
46   *Wik* (1996), p. 67
47   *Wik* (1996), p. 205
48   *Wik* (1996), p. 75
49   *Wik* (1996), p. 78
50   *Wik* (1996), p. 225
51   *Wik* (1996), p. 225
52   *Wik* (1996), p. 82
53   *Wik* (1996), p. 27
54   *Wik* (1996), p. 83

Chapter 3 – Political Games

1   Daryl Williams, Press release, 23 December 1996
2   *The Australian*, 24 December 1996
3   John Howard, Press release, 24 December 1996
4   *The Canberra Times*, 31 December 1996
5   *The Sydney Morning Herald*, 11 January 1997
6   *The Canberra Times*, 1 March 1997
7   *The Canberra Times*, 1 March 1997
8   *The Canberra Times*, 19 February 1997
9   *The Australian*, 11 January 1997
10   *The Courier Mail*, 15 January 1997
11   *The Financial Review*, 20 January 1997
12   *The Financial Review*, 6 February 1997
13   *The Australian*, 8 February 1997
14   *The Australian*, 20 February 1997
15   *The Courier Mail*, 27 February 1997
16   *The Australian*, 3 March 1997
17   *The Australian*, 14 April 1997
18   Author interview with Rick Farley, 18 June 1997
19   Frank Brennan, *One Land, One Nation: Mabo – Towards 2001*, UQP, Queensland, 1995, pp. 52–3
20   Brennan, p. 192
21   *The Australian Financial Review*, 5 February 1997
22   *The Australian Financial Review*, 14 April 1997
23   *The Weekend Australian*, 12 April 1997
24   Australian Associated Press (AAP), 22 January 1997
25   *The Age*, 10 February 1997
26   AAP, 10 March 1997
27   *The Financial Review*, 21 March 1997
28   *The Australian*, 11 April 1997
29   *The Financial Revie w*, 15 April 1997
30   *The Australian*, 16 April 1997
31   *The Australian*, 16 April 1997
32   AAP 1 May 1997
33   *The Financial Review*, 21 April 1997
34   AAP, 22 April 1997
35   *The Sydney Morning Herald*, 22 April 1997
36   *The Sydney Morning Herald*, 3 May 1997
37   Author interview with adviser to parliamentary secretary, Nick Minchin, 23 July 1997
38   Author interview with native title adviser to John Howard, 18 June 1997
39   Daryl Williams, second reading speech, *Native Title Act Amendment Bill, 1997*, 4 September 1997, p. 13
40   Author interview, 14 August 1997
41   Brian Stacey, coordinator ATSIC Wik team, Preliminary Critique of *Native Title Act* amendments, July 1997, p. 13

42   Daryl Williams, second reading speech, *Native Title Act Amendment Bill, 1997*, 4 September 1997, p. 10

43   Author interview with native title adviser to John Howard, 18 June 1997

44   *The Sydney Morning Herald*, 3 May 1997

45   John Howard, Press conference, Canberra, 28 April 1997

46   Noel Pearson, *The Australian*, 24 December 1996

47   John Connolly and Partners discussion paper, Draft Communications Plan – Influencing Response to the Wik Case, March 1997

48   Press release, Aboriginal and Torres Strait Islander Commission, 14 February 1997

49   Rick Farley, Finding a way through Wik, *The Republican*, 28 March 1997

50   National Indigenous Working Group on Native Title discussion paper, 'Coexistence – Negotiation and Certainty', April 1997. Other Aborigines may hold different views, but this is the official position.

51   NFF Aboriginal Affairs Taskforce chairman, John Mackenzie, Press release, 17 April 1997

52   *The Canberra Times*, 19 April 1997

53   *The Sydney Morning Herald*, 19 April 1997

54   *The Canberra Times*, 20 April 1997

55   Alan Ramsey, *The Sydney Morning Herald*, 3 May 1997

56   ABC Radio, 9 May 1997. See Appendix 2 for a list of the largest pastoral leaseholders in the country.

57   Network 10, *Meet the Press*, 25 May 1997

58   *The Sydney Morning Herald*, 16 May 1997

59   Australian Law Reform Commission, *Draft Comments on the Native Title Amendment Bill 1997*, published on the ALRC home page, 9 January 1998, p.1

60   *The Sydney Morning Herald*, 2 December 1997

61   *The Sydney Morning Herald*, 6 December 1997

62   Gareth Evans, speech to NFF entitled 'The Labor Party and the Farm Community', 12 August 1997

Appendix 1

Timeline

1992

June: The High Court delivers the Mabo judgement, ruling that native title survived white colonisation.

1993

June: The Wik people make a claim over pastoral leases on Cape York, and are joined by the Thayorre people.

December: The *Native Title Act* passed and becomes law.

1994

January: The National Native Title Tribunal comes into being.

May: Federal Labor Budget allocates $1.46 billion over 10 years to a land acquisition fund for dispossessed Aboriginal people

1995

February: The High Court's Brandy decision invalidates the National Native Title Tribunal's decision-making process, restricting its role to mediation.

March: The High Court rejects Western Australia's challenge to the *Native Title Act*.

June: The grave of Eddie Mabo is desecrated in Townsville.

September: Keating releases legislation to deal with procedural problems in the *Native Title Act*, including the effect of Brandy.

1996

January: The Federal Court rejects the Wik claim. The Wik appeal to a full bench and the case is removed to the High Court.

March: The Liberal Party, led by John Howard, wins a landslide election victory.

May: Howard rejects calls from the states and his backbench for legislation to extinguish native title on pastoral leases.

October: The Dunghutti people of Crescent Head, northern NSW, sign an agreement and become the first successful native title claimants under the *Native Title Act*.

23 December: The High Court hands down its decision in the Wik case. States and pastoralists demand legislation and certainty, and the National Farmers' Federation announces the death of Aboriginal reconciliation.

National Party leader Tim Fischer criticises the High Court for being activist.

1997

1 January: Howard goes on summer holidays leaving Fischer as acting Prime Minister.

3 January: Chief Justice Gerard Brennan writes to Fischer saying his attacks on the High Court were damaging, and asking him to consider whether they were 'conducive to good government'.

22 January: Howard meets Premiers and Chief Ministers. 10-point plan being developed from this date.

28 January: Howard establishes the Wik Taskforce in the Department of Prime Minister and Cabinet.

2 February: The Queensland Government, in response to Wik, freezes any substantial development of pastoral leases, the issue of new mining leases and the renewal of most existing mining leases.

3 February: Howard meets the Minerals Council of Australia and they ask him to validate all post-1994 leases. The executive director, Dick Wells, says certainty can be achieved without extinguishment of native title.

5 February: States formulate their discussion paper on native title, demanding, among other things, a 1 January 2000 deadline for claims and legislation extinguishing native title.

Howard meets ATSIC head Gatjil Djerrkura and asks him to supply a definition of native title.

6 February: Aboriginal negotiators tell Howard extinguishment would create divisions and scars. Howard sets a deadline of four weeks for a solution.

7 February: National Party crisis: President Donald McDonald issues policy statement calling for extinguishment and compensation, raising taxes if necessary to cope. Fischer says clear-cut legislation is required. Fischer also calls the High Court's decision 'judicial activism writ awful.'

Howard's parliamentary secretary in charge of native title, Nick Minchin, says 'the principles of the *Racial Discrimination Act* are important, but that does not mean the actual wording is sacrosanct.'

14 February: Round table meeting of pastoral, industry and indigenous groups, called by Howard. Howard sets a deadline of Easter for a resolution.

Northern Territory Chief Minister Shane Stone calls Northern Land Council chairman Galarrwuy Yunupingu 'just another whingeing black' for his stance on native title.

18 February: Queensland Premier Rob Borbidge announces his proposed amendments to the High Court, saying the Court is an embarrassment. He wants: fixed terms for judges; a state veto over appointments; a new judicial watchdog; referendums to sack judges.

19 February: Howard rules out any changes to the Court.

20 February: President of the Queensland National Party, David Russell, calls for leasehold land to be converted into freehold, because leasehold is an anachronism and no longer suited to 'modern pastoral husbandry and land management'.

28 February: Howard backs Fischer's attack on the High Court, saying it had become too activist.

1 March: National Party federal executive meeting. Fischer facing leadership rumblings. The federal president, Don McDonald, says the 'whole nation is on the brink of closing down' because of Wik.

6 March: National Farmers' Federation and ATSIC meet to discuss native title.

10 March: Howard says Wik is his hardest problem.

13 March: Under pressure from primary industry groups, Queensland ends its freeze on Wik-related land dealings, issuing some of the 1400 pastoral and mining leases held up.

18 March: A 'heated' National Party meeting at which Queensland Senator Bill O'Chee threatens to resign from the party if it votes to codify native title rights and not extinguish them.

19 March: The National Party executive demands extinguishment, saying codification is a 'legal minefield'.

20 March: The National Farmers' Federation launches its TV advertising campaign on all major stations.

Howard meets the state premiers at the Lodge and puts to them the earliest version of his proposed solution, but gets no agreement. He agrees to consider premiers' positions.

21 March: After the premiers' conference, Howard announces he expects an agreed solution in two weeks.

24 March: Aborigines threaten to walk away from the process after seeing some details of the Howard package, including a physical connection test, and ruling out the right to negotiate on pastoral leases.

25 March: Aboriginal negotiators refuse to have any further dealings with the NFF because of its advertising campaign.

Series of meetings between government and others in an attempt to beat Easter deadline.

26 March: Federal National Party Minister John Anderson expresses alarm at rising passions on the subject in the wake of the NFF advertisements.

30 March: Easter. Still no resolution.

11 April: Howard's plan announced as a '7-point plan'.

National Party state conference in Goondiwindi. National Party's Queensland director, Ken Crooke, says Pauline Hanson's party could cost the Queensland Government power.

13 April: The Minerals Council rejects a plan to abolish the right to negotiate on pastoral leases (or reduce it to the same limited procedural rights enjoyed by pastoralists), saying it will mean long delays in court.

Only three of 200 delegates stand to applaud Fischer at the Queensland party conference.

14 April: Howard says extinguishment is still on the table and Fischer says he is 'batting' for extinguishment. Bill

O'Chee and fellow Queensland Nationals Bob Katter, De-Anne Kelly, Paul Neville all criticise Howard.

Aborigines deliver their full response to Wik, saying they will not accept the government's plan, and suggesting a 6-point plan of their own.

15 April: Cabinet meets on Wik. Taskforce-developed 7-point plan put to them. It grows to 10 points in an attempt to win greater support from Queensland Nationals and Aborigines. Howard promises not to sell pastoralists short.

16 April: Aboriginal negotiators outline their position in a press conference.

17 April: The NFF rejects the Aboriginal position.

18 April: Aborigines and Howard meet again. Aboriginal negotiators' patience has run out. They call what they know of the plan 'virtual extinguishment,' warning of a compensation bill, a UN action and trade sanctions.

19 April: Fischer calls the Aboriginal threats a betrayal of Australians.

20 April: National Party president Don McDonald says as long as the 10-point plan presents extinguishment and exclusive land rights to pastoralists, the party will look at it.

22 April: Borbidge describes the plan as 'cute' and maintains his push for extinguishment.

Pauline Hanson's book, *The Truth*, says Aborigines had been cannibals.

24 April: The Labor NSW Premier, Bob Carr, says he is 'disposed to support' the 10-point plan.

25 April: The Australian Institute of Valuers and Land Economists says native title poses no threat to land management or planning on pastoral leases.

28–29 April: Howard meets the premiers before a Cabinet meeting expected to finalise the plan.

30 April: Aborigines see, for the first time, Howard's full 10-point plan.

1 May: Borbidge Government tables legislation to allow 3000 leaseholders to convert 22 million hectares, or 15 per cent of Queensland, to freehold by taking interest free government loans, or getting 25 per cent discount for cash purchase.

Howard meets 20 members of the Coalition Aboriginal affairs committee to explain the 10-point plan. They do not endorse it, but also do not reject it.

National Indigenous Working Group suspends further discussions with Howard, claiming a lack of good faith.

Howard publicly releases his 10-point plan saying it meets the interests of all parties.

2 May: Fischer says Howard's plan goes 'a very long way down that path' to extinguishment.

6 May: Queensland Independent and holder of the balance of power, Liz Cunningham, rejects the National Party's freehold Bill, saying too many MPs had conflicts of interest because they stood to gain too much.

Century Zinc announces its mine will go ahead after the local Aborigines sign a negotiated agreement.

Howard says his budget will cut through the 'fog' of Wik, media ownership, Pauline Hanson and Mal Colston's travel claims.

7 May: Cabinet agrees to underwrite 75 per cent of any compensation claim for native title on the condition lease-holders pay a betterment fee.

8 May: Howard explicitly attacks Pauline Hanson.

9 May: Mick Dodson attacks the pastoralists and threatens a campaign of litigation if the plan comes into effect.

12 May: NSW backbencher Ian Causley says Fischer's leadership is under challenge.

13 May: Federal Budget day.
Meeting of Coalition backbench committee on native title. Fischer's critics fail to bring their criticisms into the room.
First drafting instructions for the amendment to the *Native Title Act* go to the Office of Parliamentary Counsel.

15 May: ATSIC deputy chairman 'Sugar' Ray Robinson proposes allowing the extinguishment of native title on family farms by upgrading to freehold.
Aboriginal landowners at a summit in the Kimberley set fire to a copy of the 10-point plan.
Fischer faces down his party room by challenging his critics to challenge him.

17 May: Howard is jeered and cat-called at a pastoralists' meeting in Longreach.

18 May: Howard re-opens the goods and services tax debate.

20 May: Results of Stolen Generations inquiry, *Bringing Them Home*, leaked in *The Sydney Morning Herald*.
Borbidge accepts the 10-point plan, saying he has to face reality.

21 May: Aboriginal negotiators brief a group of foreign diplomats in Canberra on Wik.
Daryl Williams rejects compensation on stolen children, saying 'It would be wrong to judge the past by the standards of today.'

25 May: Chairman of the Council for Aboriginal Reconciliation, Pat Dodson, says the Wik plan is equivalent to the poisoning of waterholes and is about extinguishing title.

26–28 May: Aboriginal Reconciliation Convention in Melbourne. Howard refuses to apologise for the stolen children on behalf of Australia because to do so 'has significant legal implications'.

28 May: Beazley cries in parliament over the stolen generations report, and is unable to read excerpts.

New Liberal Senator, Ross Lightfoot, says in the Senate that Aborigines 'in their native state are the lowest colour on the civilisation spectrum'. Howard forces him to retract, which he does, saying, just hours later, he no longer believes it.

10 June: Ross Lightfoot joins the Coalition's backbench Aboriginal Affairs committee.

13 June: A working draft of the legislation to amend the *Native Title Act* goes to Howard.

16 June: Howard begins consultations on the working draft of the amendments.

27 June: Howard publicly releases his exposure draft of the amendments.

4 September: *Native Title Act* amendments, consisting of 300 pages, tabled in the House of Representatives. Attorney-General Daryl Williams says the legislation 'balances and gives voice to the interests of all parties'.

22 September: Independent Senator Mal Colston announces he will not attend any Senate sittings for the rest of the year, due to illness, throwing the balance of power onto Brian Harradine.

15 October: Cheryl Kernot defects to the Labor Party. Polls immediately start showing Labor ahead of the Government.

19 October: A National Indigenous Working Group delegation to South Africa says the 10-Point plan is racist.

20 October: South African President Nelson Mandela offers to mediate a resolution to Wik. Howard turns him down.

27 October: Report of the Government-dominated legal and constitutional committee tabled, recommending few changes. The minor parties dissent.

29 October: Government's legislation passes the House of Representatives. Three National Party MPs cross the floor to vote with Pauline Hanson and others to toughen it.

1 November: Patrick Dodson signals he is resigning as chairman of the Council for Aboriginal Reconciliation.

3 November: Noel Pearson calls Howard and his Government 'racist scum'.

4 November: Church leaders criticise the Government's legislation.

7 November: Howard attacks church leaders and confirms his willingness to go to a double dissolution election on Wik.

25 November: Senate debate begins. Labor and the minor parties introduce hundreds of amendments. Brian Harradine says the legislation will require 'substantial amendment'.

26 November: Nick Minchin and Tim Fischer reintroduce to the debate the furphy that backyards are under threat.

30 November: Howard addresses the nation on ABC TV saying 'The time has come to fix this issue and fix it now'.

1 December: Senator Brian Harradine votes down the six-year sunset clause on native title claims.

2 December: Harradine produces the rest of his amendments, calling them the 'essential minimum for justice and fairness'.

5 December: Amended *Native Title Act* passes the Senate after 56 hours of debate. Howard announces the Government will reject the changes.

6 December: Special Saturday sitting of the House of Representatives rejects Senate amendments.

1998

March: Second-round Senate debate expected on the Government's legislation.

October 29: Last day on which a double dissolution election can be called.

Appendix 2

Australia's biggest landholders

Private

1. Hugh MacLachlan
4.7 million ha
29 properties, mainly in SA and WA. Holdings include the world's largest sheep property. Part of a huge MacLachlan family holding. His cousin is the former NFF president and now Liberal Defence Minister Ian McLachlan, who also has significant holdings.

2. McDonald family
3.1 million ha
One of Australia's oldest rural dynasties. Nine properties in Qld's gulf country. The largest individual cattle producers in the country. Donald McDonald is the Federal President of the National Party.

3. Brian Oxenford
2.3 million ha
Nine properties in NT and Qld.

4. Ashley Daley
1.2 million ha
Three properties in Qld's channel country.

5. Peter Managazzo
1 million ha
Three properties around Normanton in Qld.

6. A. J and P. A. McBride
1 million ha
One of SA's major landholders with nine properties. Other parts of the McBride family own seven other properties, also in SA.

7. Charles Lund
0.9 million ha
Three properties in Qld, one near Alice Springs in NT.

8. E. G. Green and Sons
0.8 million ha
Six properties in the Kimberley Ranges of WA.

9. Sir James McCusker
0.8 million ha
Seven cattle properties in WA.

10. Frank McAlary
0.8 million ha
Sydney-based QC, Frank McAlary. Two properties in the Kimberley, three in NSW. McAlary was identified as the man most likely to be the mystery dancing man in the 1945 photo of people celebrating the end of the war in Sydney.

Other notable private landholders: John B. and Tim Fairfax, 11 properties, 59 000 ha; Rupert Murdoch's nephew Paddy Handbury, six properties, 62 000 ha.

Corporate

1. Aboriginal Land Trusts
20 million ha
101 properties, mainly in WA and NT, but also in
NSW, Qld, SA.

2. S. Kidman and Co
11.7 million ha
Family, formerly owned 4 per cent of Australia. 17
huge properties in Qld, SA, WA, NSW. Family worth
$70m.

3. Stanbroke Pastoral Company
10.1 million ha
Owned by the AMP Society, 27 properties across Qld
and NT. The nation's biggest beef producer, with more
than 350 000 head of cattle.

4. Austag
6.4 milllion ha
Bought by Elders in 1995 for $161 million, 16
properties in Qld and NT.

5. North Australian Pastoral Company
6 million ha
14 Properties across Qld and NT.

6. Heytesbury Pastoral Company
5.6 million ha
Janet Holmes a Court's company, 19 properties in WA,
Qld, NT. The third-biggest beef producer. She is rated
by *Business Review Weekly* to be worth $250m.

7. Consolidated Pastoral Company
4.5 million ha
Owned by Kerry Packer. Australia's fourth-biggest
beef producer. 14 properties across northern Australia.
Also owns five abattoirs.

8. Queensland and Northern Territory Pastoral Company
2.7 million ha
Owned by Bankers' Trust. 12 properties worth $150 million.

9. Tipperary (Indonesia)
1.9 million ha
Owned by an Indonesian company, Bakire and Brothers, eight NT properties.

10. Colinta Holdings
1.2 million ha
A subsidiary of Mount Isa Mines. Seven NT and Qld properties.

Other notable corporate owners: National Mutual, 0.8 million ha; BHP Minerals, 0.7 million ha; the Sultan of Brunei, 0.6 million ha; Rupert Murdoch's News Limited, 0.15 million ha.

This information was researched and compiled by the *Australian Farm Journal* and is reproduced by permission. It appeared in Volume 6, No. 9, November 1996.

Index

Other titles of interest
from Hyland House ...

~ Current Affairs ~

Save Our ABC: The Case for Maintaining Australia's National Broadcaster
Edited by Morag Fraser and Joseph O'Reilly
Prominent Australians such as Robert Hughes, Phillip Adams, Frank Brennan and Robert Manne eloquently argue the case for the ABC's future.
ISBN 1 875657 99 1, $14.95 pbk

Putting the People Last: Government, Services and Rights in Victoria
Edited by Michael Webber with Mary L. Crooks
A critical examination of the Kennett government's record in Victoria on health, civil liberties, education and privatisation. ISBN 1 875657 82 7, $29.95 pbk

~ Aboriginal Literature and History ~

The Indigenous Literature of Australia: Milli Milli Wangka
Mudrooroo
An unique, fascinating and sometimes controversial examination of Aboriginal literature, from the songlines of prehistory through to the novels, songs and poetry of today. ISBN 1 86447 47 9, $24.95 pbk

My Dear Spencer: The Letters of F. J. Gillen to Baldwin Spencer
Edited by John Mulvaney, Howard Morphy & Alison Petch
The pioneering work performed by Gillen and Spencer in studying the indigenous life of Central Australia is recorded in these fascinating and highly readable letters, which have lain unpublished for a hundred years. ISBN 1 86447 021 6, $49.95 hdbk

You Are What You Make Yourself to Be: the Story of a Victorian Aboriginal Family, 1842-1980
Phillip Pepper with Tess de Araugo
The moving and unforgettable story of one Aboriginal family's experience of the impact of white settlement. ISBN 0 947062 60 2, $19.95 pbk

Hyland House Publishing Pty Ltd
Publishers of Quality Australian Books since 1976
'Hyland House', 387–389 Clarendon Street, South Melbourne, Victoria 3205
Tel: (03) 9696 9064 Fax: (03) 9696 9065 E-mail: hyland@peg.apc.org
Internet: www.peg.apc.org/~hyland